To Sheila

Growin' Up

One Scouser's Social History, 1925–1942

Johnnie Woods

Copyright © John Woods, 1989

First published in 1989 by Carnegie Press

This edition published by Palatine Books,
an imprint of Carnegie Publishing Ltd
Carnegie House,
Chatsworth Road,
Lancaster, LA1 4SL
www.carnegiepublishing.com

ISBN 1-874181-23-3

Typeset by Carnegie Publishing
Printed and bound in the UK by Cromwell Press, Trowbridge

Contents

Acknowledgements

I would like to thank all the people, both family and friends, who have shown interest and gave help when I decided to commit my memories to paper. I would like to extend a special 'thank you' to my daughter for her unstinting clerical efforts. Above all, however, I would like to pay tribute to the people of my pre-war Scotland Road, some of whom alas now long dead, for their guts, their rough dignity and their tenacity. Their humour alone shone brightly through what could have been a harrowing childhood.

Liverpool 1989

Note on the illustrations

The publishers would like to extend their grateful thanks to all the staff at the Liverpool Record Office for their help in tracing many of the old photographs used in this book (marked as LIV.R.O.). Their help has been invaluable. We would also like to thank Liverpool Libraries and Information Services for their kind permission to reproduce them here. Other photographs were by the author and from the family collection.

Chapter One

The street

It seems like a statement of the obvious to say it was bad luck to be born into a poor home in the mid 'twenties; it could be seen as a double blow to be born into the poverty of Bostock Street, Scotland Road, where most families fought their own private battles against destitution.

The street itself, Bostock or 'Bosi' as it was known to us all, was a tiny, narrow cobbled affair, only about five yards wide from pavement to pavement and no more than one hundred and fifty yards long. On each of its corners with Scotland Road stood the pubs, Joe Allen's and Duffy's[1] both owned by Walkers; on the corners with Great Homer Street there was yet another pub, this time owned by Bents', and Lunts' cake shop.

A Liverpool back street, not dissimilar to those I knew as a young boy. (LIV.R.O.)

The Europa pub in the 1980s, situated at the top of Bostock Street, or 'Bosi' as everyone called it. Scotland Road is now a dual carriageway leading to the town centre and tunnel. Most of the old houses have long since gone.

Looking from Scottie Road towards Great Homer, the left-hand side of 'Bosi' was made up mostly of terraced back-to-backs, with two stables in the middle.[2] Towards the end of the street was the mission hall, which housed a variety of enterprises over the years, Greenwoods' paint firm and a stable/coal merchant's. On the other side there was our general shop owned by Mr Simmcock[3] and a 'hollow' facing the hall; no one was quite sure why this piece of flat land was there but the general consensus was that there had once been a couple of houses on the site which had just fallen down through neglect. Again there were the usual terraced houses, with Mrs Boardman's being known as the 'cookhouse'.

The street, like so many others in Liverpool, reflected the town's religious divide, the top or Scotland Road end being mainly Catholic, the bottom Protestant, predominantly Church of England. Being Catholic by birth, if not inclination, my social circle mainly revolved around the families at the top.[4]

Looking back, I would guess that up to two hundred children lived in the street in the 'twenties and 'thirties; one did not go short of mates.

Our play area was limited but improvisation was the order of the day; we lads would play football with bundles of paper tied with string if we had no ball and the entries[5] were our goalposts. In true English tradition, we played cricket, jamming the sewer manholes in the middle of the street with bits of wood as makeshift stumps. Rounders, too, was a favourite, the steps of designated houses being the bases, not always a popular decision with their occupants.

The girls played jacks and hollies, hop scotch and, naturally, skipping. Spinning tops were envied toys. The girls seemed to have more imagination than the boys, playing 'shop' and using broken crockery or 'banie mugs' as money; the bigger the piece, the greater its worth, the most valuable being bits with gold paint. If some girls had no toys or broken plate, then there was always 'cherry wobs'. Here a child would take it in turn to throw a cherry stone up a downspout while the others had their stones in the indent in the pavement at the bottom. If a stone on its descent hit another, then it was claimed by the gleeful thrower. These stones were treasured, kept for years and even handed down to younger sisters when the elder girls decided that childhood was over.

For the most part we were happy and ignorant, most especially of our parents' struggle against poverty and unemployment. Like Norman Tebbit's dad, all looked for jobs which, in Liverpool at least, rarely existed. Most houses were overcrowded, with several generations of family members, and it was one's accepted lot to provide for the aged and infirm.

Bostock Street in the 1980s. Approximately where the second tree stands was the house where I lived in the 1930s. It is, of course, practically unrecognisable today.

Father, seated, aged around twenty-four. Often at sea for long periods, it was not until later, when he had taken a shore job, that I came to know him well. He was strict but generally his homecomings were pleasant interludes.

Our house had an attic, two bedrooms, a parlour, kitchen, outside toilet and a cold water tap in the back yard. Here in my early years lived my mother and father (when he was home from sea), my two brothers and myself and my grandmother, 'Ninny', and a great aunt; six in all.[6] The two old girls lived, ate, slept and eventually died in the parlour; here they had their enormous brass bed, brass fender and stools. They coveted all things brass.

My mother, Mary Ellen, acted as unpaid cook and bottle washer to us all and the place seemed surprisingly roomy. Then Aunt Julia's husband died of pneumonia[7] and life became more crowded as she, plus four daughters and a son, moved in with us. All the boys were relegated to the attic, the girls and Julia to the back bedroom, my mother and father in the front and the two old ones, still with the brass, in the parlour.

Despite the overcrowding, I came to respect Aunt Julia, who worked her way out of destitution by selling fruit and vegetables; she eventually got a small house above a stable in Kew Street and later moved back to a reasonably spacious three-bedroomed terrace in Bostock Street. Given the lack of the protection later available in the post-war Welfare State, her achievements were remarkable and all her children were a credit to her unstinting efforts.

During these early, noisy years, one of my earliest and most vivid memories was Ninny's funeral. My brothers and I were terrified of the coffin, the glass-sided hearse and even the driver who, with his top hat and whip, did not look too sociable. We and the other relatives were conveyed by horse-drawn cabs; what surprised me most was the behaviour of the neighbours; as was common practice,

Aunt Julia with three of her daughters and son John in the background. When her husband died, they all moved in with us, leading to even greater overcrowding. I developed great respect for Aunt Julia, who grafted her way out of poverty by sheer hard work and determination. This picture was taken in 1929. I am standing at the front. The two other boys were my brothers, both now deceased.

the street was lined with bareheaded acquaintances and friends, silently saying their last goodbyes.

We slowly made our way to Ford cemetery which, then as now, was pretty grim; the rain came down in sheets as we shivered by the graveside and I prayed genuinely, probably for the first time, to be home as soon as possible. The whole thing could indeed have taken much less time, as the undertakers were changing over to motor cars, but the old girl had stipulated before her death, like many others, that she was to go by horse because it took longer to get to Ford.

Thus, at four, I was introduced to the working-class rituals of death. Like all streets, 'Bosi' had its woman, in our case Mrs Mullen, to wash and lay out the corpse. She would then drape white sheets around the windows and arrange any flowers. When all was ready, people would visit, pray and chat around the coffin; all this could last for up to three days depending on the day of the week and the demands on priests and undertakers.

Neighbours held collections for wreaths and, if necessary, for help towards the funeral costs. As ever, working-class people had their rigid standards of self-respect and the fear of a pauper's burial haunted many a pensioner's nightmares. From 1930 to 1942 I do not remember anyone in 'Bosi' suffering this final act of indignity as all would give what they had to avoid resort to the authorities. If you gave money in this way it was never to be mentioned even if, the very next week, there was one of the regular street rows.

The year 1930 was also momentous for my first serious bout of illness. We all caught scarletina, very common and contagious among kids of our social class. The side-effects were fascinating to small boys; all your skin seemed to peel off from finger to toe nails as you were delirious with a raging temperature. The two visits by our local doctor later played their part in my early political education. On each occasion the old skinflint demanded cash payments before he would even look at us; on the second call my mother was two pennies short and ran to borrow from a neighbour. In the event he prescribed nothing and merely told her to do what she already knew, to keep the curtains drawn, the room temperature steady and to wipe our foreheads. She should have asked for a refund.

As infancy drew to a close and school loomed ahead, in illness I somehow acquired my most treasured possession, a baby's dummy, sucked surreptitiously when my mother's back was turned. She had long since taken such things from me. Later in life a doctor friend said it was my security – the death, the illness and my father's long absences at sea had taken their toll. Luckily at the time I just basked in my cosy ignorance and thought myself to be quite a tough little nipper.

Chapter Two

Early days at school

The world altered dramatically with my first day at school. I dutifully turned up with my mother and other kids and mums at the entrance to St Anthony's Roman Catholic school, my *alma mater*, and was confronted by a huge woman in black robes with an enormous black and white hat; swinging from her waist were the statutory crucifix and rosary beads. I immediately decided she was my first real monster.

Parents visibly cowered before her; issuing instructions in a booming voice, she proceeded to extricate each child from his parent. I watched, open mouthed with terror, as most were crying, some urinating and all verged on mass hysteria. I decided I would not go down without a struggle. When she reached me, I clung to my mother's skirt. I am not sure what happened next, but I know I kicked and she won – my first and last fight with a nun.

I was then herded with the rest along a dingy passageway; instinctively I had put my hand in my jersey and frantically retrieved the dummy, hanging as always on a string around my neck. I had only had it in my mouth for a few reassuring seconds when the monster spotted it. Like lightning she grabbed out. I thought she was going to pull off my head. After one quick tug, out came her scissors and that was the last of the dummy. I succumbed to my fate and the education system and silently wet myself. A temporary reprieve came with the dinner break when the monster had words with my long-suffering mother about my 'antics'. It was later left up to my brothers to drag me back to school.

The monster turned out to be Sister Mary, headmistress of the infants and, despite first encounters, kindness itself. I still swear she was at least six foot eight and I was always staggered by the way she remembered all the children and their parents; to the local Catholic community she was a real lady.

School naturally broadened my horizons; friendships were struck with kids from other streets; some were better off, others not. All were characters. We seemed remarkably unimpressed by our relative poverty. Most wore pumps in all weathers. If we played football, some would lend their boots or if they were really well-off, brought a spare pair for a mate.

As we struggled through the 'three Rs' we had exams and I remember with more pride now than then coming first and getting a copy of *Robinson Crusoe* as a prize. Life seemed to get more interesting by the day; I was pronounced bright, missed

St Anthony's Church on Scotland Road, built in the then fashionable style in 1833.

out the Juniors and went straight into the 'big boys'.[1] Here there were two classes,
A and B; at first I entered the B stream taught by Miss Duffy.[2] I really liked her but
she seemed to spend most of her time sending me, no doubt a bored nuisance, on
messages. At eleven each morning I would go for two wholemeal cobs; she insisted
on triangular ones from Lunts.[3] She would always want some cheese but did not

care where I bought it as long as it was cheap. After a while all this became quite dull so for a laugh I would ask shopkeepers to cut the cheese into triangles to fit the cobs; some were daft or kind enough to try; others chased me.

Soon my daily routine was upset when I noticed I was being watched by a man, an 'outsider' with a collar and tie and black suit. Eventually he approached me.

'What school are you at?'

'St Anthony's,' I replied, suspiciously.

'But it's a quarter past eleven and your dinnertime's not till twelve!' he said, moving as if to grab me.

I was off like a shot; it was the schools' attendance officer, enemy of all truants and a few of my closest colleagues. I thought, 'I'll give you a run for your money.' I ran across Scotland Road skipping between tram cars with a certain flair. I legged it down Kew Street, through the entry and along Newsham Street. All the time he followed, puffing and panting. Every now and again I stopped, letting him nearly catch up and then off again. I dashed into school; he hesitated momentarily and then entered. Deliberately I ran screaming into Miss Atkinson's class, 'There's a man chasing me!'

Pandemonium ensued, Miss Atkinson protective and bellowing, the bloke yelling he was from the school board. When she realised I was not in her class, the officer looked jubilant, insisting I had been sagging. I explained I was in Miss Duffy's class, who came and gave evidence in my defence. She was somewhat suspicious and asked

St. Anthony's School and Social Club, where the old school stood.

An old Avery tram car. One of the real 'Bone Rattlers', now in Pier Head Large Objects
Museum. These trams really were not one of the most comfortable modes of transport ever.

A considerable improvement were the (modestly) upholstered seats of the Green Goddess trams. This one, now also in the museum, was the last tram seen in Liverpool, in 1956.

I, as a 'clever dick', was moved into Miss Atkinson's class. She was a great teacher and we used to visit her in this house in Sylvester Street.

why I had not explained to the man in Scotland Road. 'He never asked,' I replied. It seemed to do the trick as they all laughed in mutual embarrassment.

The next term I, as a 'clever dick' was moved into Miss Atkinson's class; with more humour than most she looked behind me as I entered. 'Just checking there's no one chasing you this time,' she chuckled. She was an excellent teacher given the constraints of the school and her charges. She was very good at art and developed in many of us talents of which we were unaware. She lived locally in a red-brick house in Sylvester Street and did not seem to mind if a couple of us dropped in. She showed us how to paint, draw and mix colours. Once I told her I had decided to be a real painter. 'Do what you like within the law; if it be painting, so be it,' she replied somberly, no doubt realising what little chance most of us had.[4]

By now it was summer 1934 and the headmaster of the seniors, Big Murray, told us that King George V and Queen Mary were coming to Liverpool in the July to open the Mersey Tunnel. We had all watched it being built and during our next art lesson Miss Atkinson asked us to draw something in our mind's eye. I alone chose the tunnel; with some pride she dispatched me plus picture to Murray's office. He chatted for a while and then asked if I had ever seen the King. I looked at him as though he was mad as he proposed to get me a seat to see the opening. I was not that keen on the whole idea as I had a horrible feeling it would involve dressing up.

A horse and cart on Tithebarn Street in 1918. (LIV.R.O.)

This would be expensive for my mother; most of my clothes were well worn and patched and I remembered the last such torment two years before at my first communion.

Mr Murray did, however, honour his promise and I was duly installed among a crowd of adults by St John's Gardens to see the King and Queen. God knows how, but my mother had even acquired my first suit of dark blue serge and togged me out with collar and tie, white shirt, grey stockings and black shoes.[5]

Uncomfortably I watched the early stages of pomp and ceremony. Like most little boys, I soon became incredibly bored; I was relieved from this state by a sharp poke in the back. There my 'bessie mate', Eddie, whispered that some well-meaning WI types were distributing boxes of King George V chocolates to poor kids in Exchange Flags. We ducked through the crowds, across St John's Lane, along Victoria Street, up Stanley Street into Dale Street and then ran up Moorfields, down Tithebarn Street into Exchange Flags.

My pal explained that our gang had got two 'stirring carts'[6] hidden out of view in George Street; there, sure enough, several small lads were busy loading dozens of boxes of royal chocs, resplendent with a picture of George V surrounded by laurel leaves. It seemed like the easiest scam we had ever pulled; the same scruffy kids rejoining the queue of children to tables stacked with goodies. They had all been

Eldon Street (just off Vauxhall).

through at least twice but 'clothes maketh a man' and on my third attempt, a well-spoken female voice said loudly,

'I'm sure you've already been through!'

There was nothing else to do but agree as I realised too late how I must have stuck out like a clean and tidy sore thumb. Suspicions aroused, the gang agreed to get back to base as quickly as possible before our haul was discovered. We, plus carts and loot, sped up George Street, past the Stadium, through St Paul's Square and the 'Tunnel of Love',[7] into Pall Mall, up Leeds Street, along Vauxhall Road and finally to 'Bosi'. Here we had our beloved den.[8]

So much for my privileged presence at an historical event! Needless to say I had to use my imagination to the full when quizzed by Big Murray. In fact it became more routine for me to see Murray for the cane.

I, along with several others, had to pass a blacksmith's, Harper's, on the way to school. The sights and sounds were fascinating: the fire, the bellows, the smelting metal, the hammering and the huge carthorses waiting to be shod. We would sometimes find a couple of horseshoe nails and make them into makeshift darts by putting tar around them and finishing them off with a couple of pigeon feathers. We would then use them on a wooden gate where we chalked our target.

Understandably, this resulted in late arrival at school, and Big Murray was not a head to tolerate such behaviour; latecomers and other varieties of miscreants were sent to queue outside his office for his version of pastoral care. Sometimes you would just get one smack of the cane on the palm of your hand, but the regulars were treated to as many whacks as Murray deemed necessary.

So we all waited, in cocky, boastful terror, in the long dim passageway that led to his room; the victim would knock, enter and come out and down the other side of the passage, hugging a stinging hand and fighting back unboyish tears.

One lad, Denny McCarthy, proved to be for a while my salvation. When he was in with Murray he would drive the head close to clinical insanity by moving his hand persistently at the very last minute. After two or three goes, Murray would grab the shrieking McCarthy by the wrist with one hand and try to cane him with the other. This regular wrestling bout allowed a couple of us at the top of the queue to quickly jump across the passage and walk down the other side, pretending to have received our just rewards. The trouble was that too many tried the ploy too often and Murray, who was no fool, soon began to count us as he came in. One morning two of us were daft to try it once too often. Murray had done his count, knew all of us well and at ten o'clock strolled purposefully into our classroom. A serious, stern lecture followed, although I was not sure if he definitely knew the culprits. I was chosen to get a cane from his office; the room

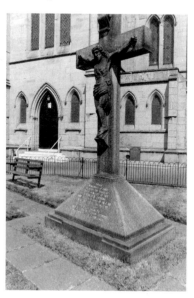

Monument to the boys from St Anthony's, Scotland Road, who died in the war.

was locked but in his perverse humour, a brand new cane was resting against the door. I returned with it only to hear Murray announce that I was the main 'dodger'; in considerable horror and much humiliation, I was forced to bend over a table and got 'seven of the best' on my backside. We never tried it on again.

Despite the canings, we all respected Murray as an excellent headmaster; the rest of the staff also won our affection; in addition to Misses Duffy and Atkinson there was Mr Hewitson, 'little Murray', Mr Carroll and 'Daddy' Lawler. The teachers did their best with a school tough by any standards and never shirked from knocking us into line when necessary. Here they had the backing of nearly all the parents to whom it was useless to moan; nine out of ten would give you more punishment if you mentioned incidents at school.

I later regretted that I invested so little in my own education; I even dodged the 'scholarship' exam despite encouragement from teachers that I would pass. Indeed their very certainty was the main reason; no way did I want to leave my mates and go to a posh school where you had to wear a 'nancy boy' uniform and, God forbid, a cap! On Scotland Road it was enough to put you in personal danger. My mother went along with my refusal, much to my father's unbelievable wrath when he came home from sea; by then it was too late, the decision had been made. Like too many others, I realised the value of education when it had slipped through my fingers and hence my efforts to encourage my own child later in life. In the 1930s there seemed too many interesting things going on to worry about tomorrow and getting on.

Chapter Three

Pawnshops and poverty

Big Murray's invitation to the opening of the Mersey Tunnel had worried me because of the cost to my mother; at my first communion two years earlier I had had to wear an awful but dear outfit, a white blouse, black velvet shorts with white pearl buttons and real shoes as opposed to the usual pumps. I had only worn it twice when it seemed, thank God, to disappear. On reflection, I realised my mother had later pawned the lot. I was quite relieved as all in our gang hated these 'cissy' clothes and most of theirs had ended up in the same shop.

Pawnshops were plentiful in the Scotland Road area but the most popular, and the one we loyally used, was owned by James O'Hare at the corner of Benledi Street, across the road from 'Bosi'. It is all but impossible for some today to imagine the poverty experienced by too many in the 1930s; we and our neighbours would pledge

Scottie and Burlington Street in 1949. The de-infestation department were often seen around here, and the council ran a dinner house which provided free dinners for the poorer kids. (LIV.R.O.)

Kew Street looking east towards Great Homer Street. On the right are the rear of Kew Street flats, with the rear of the houses on Bosi on the left. (LIV.R.O.)

anything in hard times to get food during the week. On Fridays, some might have enough earnings to redeem their belongings, only to be back at O'Hare's on Monday mornings. Husbands' suits were the most popular items; men said they had an 'indigo' suit for this very reason, 'indigo Monday', 'outdigo Friday'!

The Monday pawn sessions were good-natured occasions, Scousers, as usual, having the wit to laugh at their own misfortunes. The variety of pledges fascinated the kids, the suits, shoes, bundles of rags, bedlinen and assorted musical instruments. There was always a good deal of humorous banter about the value of a pledge. Yet the saddest times were when Mr O'Hare had sales of articles which had not been redeemed within the agreed time limits. These were usually held on the 'hollow' in Kew Street; it was truly pathetic to see people's faces as they watched their few treasured possessions sold to others.

There were various types of credit, most of which seemed in retrospect designed to exacerbate rather than alleviate poverty. Many desperate for cash would get a Sturlas, Clarkson's or Co-op. cheque which allowed them an agreed sum of instant credit on certain purchases. Therein followed weeks of repayments until the debt was honoured. Some were then crazy or hungry enough to take their newly acquired belongings straight to the pawn shop for ready cash, all in all, robbing Peter to pay

Burlington Street dwellings in 1910. Portland Gardens took their place and these in turn have been replaced by new houses! (LIV.R.O.)

Burlington Street Court, this time in 1925. Inspectors used to come round to check for over-crowding but the local residents were far too smart for them. The inspectors would begin in the cellars and people would run from level to level and house to house to avoid being spotted and counted in the tally. (LIV.R.O.)

Street urchins pose for a photograph on the Steble fountain in the city centre. (LIV.R.O.)

Paul! Some food shops did give 'tick', shopkeepers being anxious to keep their own heads above water, but prices were raised by a ha'penny or two per item. Some shops were known to cheat their customers; here our only protection was 'the weights and measures man' who did spot checks on scales and weights. Scales could be temporarily confiscated if they were faulty and, although rare, there were a few successful prosecutions.

Children seemed to be permanently hungry; sometimes kids would wait for carters or dockers or any man coming home from work and beg for left-overs from their 'carrying out'. Most would oblige and some definitely saved food for this very purpose. People thus helped out as best they could. Poverty was permanent but destitution was intermittent; we all knew the difference. I can recall the times when my father's allotment from sea was not paid on time; sometimes it could be up to a month late. Such times could defy description.

One month we were all really hungry, including the family dog, Jumbo, a friendly, scruffy mongrel. Our neighbour was one of the better off in 'Bosi' and knew of our plight. One day she shouted over the backyard wall, 'Mary Ellen, I've gorra piece of meat for Jumbo – I'll throw it over.' It landed on the roof of our outside lavatory, the best part of a leg of lamb. My mother, in some shock, frantically whispered, 'John, John, quick, quick, on the roof!' I scrambled up and retrieved the marvel which was duly chopped up with as many vegetables as we could lay our hands on; it made a great pan of 'scouse' which lasted for at least two days, the poor dog ending up with a spotless bone.

Christmas 1936 was again hard to forget; dad away at sea, mother penniless. By Christmas Day, mysteriously, we had acquired a rabbit and a big piece of beef. Much later in life, shortly before his death, one of our benefactors told me the story. On Christmas Eve he and three others had got a handcart and tied sacks around the wheels to deaden the clatter on the cobbled streets. They went in the dark to Chapel Gardens and waited until the butchers next to the Throstle's Nest pub closed. They then helped themselves to as much meat and poultry as they could grab, loaded the cart and one kept watch as the others pushed silently along Great Homer, up Newsham Street, through the entry into Kew Street and across the hollow to the back entry of 'Bosi'. Thus, as 3 a.m. on Christmas Day these erstwhile Santas distributed food parcels among the needy.

St Anthony's Church and the Throstle's Nest pub in the 1980s. The Stanley Racing shop was a butcher's in the 1930s.

David Logan, Labour MP for this area, lived above this shop which was the Taveners sweet shop in the 1930s.

There are those today who would moralise tediously about stealing from shopkeepers but these men had only the best of intentions and put themselves at no small risk for no personal gain; in better times they would never have dreamed of such action. I later made a special point of attending all their funerals as a mark of respect from a young lad whose belly was full at Christmas. If there is a God, I am sure he has forgiven my Robin Hoods.

Poverty brings other problems as well as poor clothing and empty stomachs. Burlington Street contained one testament to our living standards, in the shape of the council's disinfection department. At local schools we were regularly subjected to the ever-knowing fingers of the 'nit nurse' as she roughly examined heads for vermin. If she saw anything suspicious, you would end up down at the disinfection offices for foul smelling baths full of alien liquids and tons of carbolic soap.

Summer was a time of dread for the women; flies abounded and an additional expense on every household's budget were the fly-catchers, lengths of very sticky sellotape which hung from the ceiling for weeks to catch flies. In the end they probably caused more, not less, disease.

The real summer plague arrived with the 'bed bugs'; they would come out of the cracks in the wall in their thousands. Whole armies travelled in darkness; with a lit candle you could watch them scurry in retreat. When killed they stank; we, given the predilections of young lads, burned them with candles. Some people resorted to using paraffin blow lamps to burn them from bed springs when they had taken hold. It was later showed that the vermin were not caused by a family's failings but flourished in the poor building fabrics of our old houses; they were made of wooden laths, horsehair and plaster, an ideal breeding ground.

The extent of people's poverty tended to catch me unaware; we used to go to an Irish woman's shop, later to be Mick Daly's undertakers. Here an old lady sold cheap sweets like two 'black jacks' for a ha'penny. One day when we had bought our usual, we passed Taverner's, on the corner of Kew Street. Above the shop lived our local Labour MP, David Logan, who represented Scotland Road till he was eighty-four.[1] He asked us to get him some coal from Dutton's yard in Elias Street. Having duly accomplished our task, Mr Logan gave me a packet of five 'Woodbines'. I was only nine and took them to my mother who explained that perhaps Mr Logan thought my dad was unemployed and would be grateful for a cigarette. My mate's dad was out of work and the cigarettes were given to him. He suffered from poor health and never worked again but he had three boys and a girl.

This was my first encounter with 'police clothes', 'charity outfits' given to paupers. The boys wore them like the uniforms of depression, brown corduroy suits, a shirt, tie and clogs. They stood out for all to see, hear and smell; the clogs had steel rims and the suits gave off a terrible smell when the kids stood too close to the fire. Even their hair marked them out as different, since it was cropped leaving just a small tuft on their foreheads. Their dignity was rarely considered but most bore it with stoic good humour.

These kids were entitled to free dinners; they were issued with tickets for the 'dinner house' at the top of Burlington Street. One Saturday one of the lads said he had to go there for his dinner before we treated him to the 'Penny Rush' at the 'Derby'.[2] We volunteered to walk with him; we were not allowed in but watched the proceedings from the large door which was left open for fresh air during the meal. I was genuinely shocked; at big, long tables sat kids in rows of twenty to thirty eating what looked like crusts of stale bread with a kind of stew. Most dipped the bread to make it edible; it was the nearest I came to Dickensian England.

It seems that hypocrites, like the poor, are always among us. There were those in our little community who, like too many today, saw poverty as a punishment for personal failing, irresponsibility or inadequacy. Again, like today, many of these 'self-helpers' were pharisaical devotees of organised Christianity.

I remember once inadvertently showing my face at a Harvest Festival held in a large tent. We looked in, amazed, visibly salivating at all the gorgeous food as the righteous, upright citizens sang to their Almighty. We were soon noticed; dirty looks and sideways glances abounded; the atmosphere could have been cut with a knife. The vicar stalked down the aisle and coldly told us to disappear. 'On your way, you little scruffs. We don't want your sort in here!' I hope my Almighty reminded him of 'suffer little children, come unto me' if the old goat ever got as far as the Pearly Gates.

Nevertheless, some true Christians did exist; pauper families were always assured a Goodfellows' food parcel at Christmas, containing tinned food, fruit and perhaps sweets or a piece of meat. The 'Goodfellows' must have kept a league table of destitution as they nearly always got it right. They also honoured people's self-respect, as they delivered their presents personally after dark, to avoid the embarrassed sympathies of neighbours.

In a similar way, all we children looked forward to the 'League of Welldoers'[3] tickets for the Christmas party. The Welldoers canvassed families asking for the number of tickets required. The parties were held in Limekiln Lane, the best part being the street entertainment we provided ourselves in the queue outside. Children did comic acts, acrobatic turns and all types of vaudeville, all to come to an abrupt end as the doors opened and in we charged. We usually got a cup of cocoa, a couple of cakes and some fruit; on the way out there might be a toy. So, in spite of our neo-Victorian moralists, Scotland Road did ring out every now and again with peace and goodwill to all.

Chapter Four

'You've got to earn a penny or two!'

From a very early age we all realised the importance of earning a few pennies for our 'leisure activities'. Here Scotland Road, teeming with shops, markets and traders of all descriptions, provided numerous opportunities, both legal and sometimes not so legal, for streetwise kids. We would all be up early at weekends and during the summer and Christmas holidays to earn a few bob at the market in Great Nelson Street.

Although the place seemed to overflow with fruit and veg, on Saturdays there was a general uncovered market, full of stalls selling household wares, tacky bric-a-brac and, above all, oilcloth. I and the rest of the gang would loiter all day next to the oilcloth stalls offering to carry the stuff home for local buyers. If one or two women were doing the buying, we were usually guaranteed custom; with the men it was more touch and go. We would struggle through the busy streets, out of breath, lugging what were often very heavy rolls and then be tipped anything from three to six old pence. Total earnings varied depending on the time of year and the current economic prosperity or lack of it in the community.

Only once were we not paid. Two of us had carried with considerable verve a large roll from the market quite a fair way to Thomaston Street, right at the other end of Great Homer. Here the houses had the dreaded high steps leading up to the front door and lobby. Our male client asked us to carry the damn thing right up the steps and along the hall. Exhausted, we summoned one great last burst of energy, heaved and deposited the roll as instructed. We then smiled proudly and hovered like erstwhile waiters.

'What do you two want? Come on, on yer way!' he said.

'But people usually give us a tanner for carrying yer stuff!' we exclaimed in amazement.

'On yer way quick, yer little buggers, or I'll have yer locked up for begging!' he shouted, raising an arm in a gesture that left us in no doubt.

Off we trotted, our professional pride dented, our resentment enormous.

'Get the number of the house. We'll get him,' I said to the comrade with malevolent spite and bravado.

Revenge is ours, we thought and decided; like the Bible which had been punched into us, it would be accorded with some degree of fairness. 'An eye for an eye,' *et al*

Aerial photograph of Great Homer Street. (LIV.R.O.)

and it was agreed we would return after dark and smash one window, replacement cost at least one shilling. Miraculously, good sense prevailed as we asked a pal who lived near by in Aughton Street if he knew the mean guy. It turned out he was a police sergeant at Rose Hill police station.[1] Such knowledge immediately cancelled our plans but our ill feeling simmered for months.

One reasonably regular source of income when we were feeling organised was to chop and sell wood in bundles. As nearly all still had coal fires, it was quite a lucrative trade, although it could cause confusion as such batches of firewood were called 'chips' and many a kid sent on a message for a neighbour would return with wood instead of fried potatoes. We were quite entrepreneurial, looking back, as we would invest our earnings from wood and oilcloth in buying candles, four dozen a box, from a wholesaler's in Rose Vale. These we would sell door to door.

By sheer chance we stumbled on our most profitable source of cash; in the 1930s St Martin's Market, known as the 'Paddy's Market' to the locals, was still in Scotland Road.[2] At the end of trading stallholders would dump in a sort of skip all the old clothes, some no better than rags, which they had failed to sell. These would then be taken away by the council's binmen. The skip was in a yard at the corner of

Maddox Street and Bevington Hill which was opened very early by the market attendants for the refuse collectors.

We decided to hire a handcart, our only outlay, and get to the yard at opening time. We loaded as many clothes as we could before we were disturbed and then took them to our buyers. This developed into a regular habit for many months; we felt we were in 'the big time' as we took our wares to either Packinham's in Gordon Street or King's in William Moult Street. We never got less than ten shillings and once two pounds, princely sums in those days. We knew the 'raggies' were not giving us a fair price because we were kids, but we did not care.

Some of the 'rag tatters' who made their living at acquiring such supplies were none too happy with us; in fact two of them discovered our source and got in on the act but, for quite a while, we got our share of the bounty.

By the time I was twelve, I acquired what I considered to be my strangest Saturday job. I had started to go to the football match on Saturday afternoons and used to wait for a mate at the top of 'Bosi'. Here there was a court at the corner of which stood Harry Silverman's tailors shop; it always seemed very dark and we were all terrified of the owner.

One Saturday Harry and I started to chat and he asked me if I could go into his living quarters at the back of the shop and light his fire and gas mantle. I was worried but more perplexed and, to be honest, very nosey. I agreed suspiciously and was amazed to see a very clean living room with the fire all set with coal and wood and a chair with a box on it so I could reach the mantle. All this seemed very strange to me but nonchalantly I struck the match and got everything going. Looking at me with some amusement, Harry gave me a couple of sugar lumps and asked if I could come every Saturday. It seemed no skin off my nose and so I good-naturedly agreed.

It proved a subject of ongoing conversation that afternoon when I told the lads.

'Sounds a lazy bugger to me!' said one, summing up our general hypothesis.

'Eh mam, Harry Silverman asked me to light his gas and fire this savvy and it was all set out ready. How about that for laziness!'

'You stupid kid,' she retorted somewhat haughtily for her, 'don't yer know nothing? Harry's a good clean living Jew trying to do his best by his religion. Jew's aren't supposed to do things on Saturdays, cos it's their Sunday.'

Although this initially sounded a bit Irish to me, with a bit more explanation it made sense. I went for a few Saturdays, growing concerned about ever forgetting and letting him down. It became in a strange way a religious duty for me. After several weeks, sugar lumps and assorted rewards, Harry, who now had mellowed into quite a likeable sort, asked for my address in case he needed to get in touch.

A painting of Paddy's Market. None of this exists any more, but it shows how the old place used to look. (LIV.R.O.)

The following Monday after school, my mother said that Mr Silverman had been round and wanted to see me. He knew of a real Saturday job. I rushed round, worried about the hours and missing the match. He explained it was a delivery job for a friend of his and you finished when you had done all your deliveries. He did not know the wages and my heart sank until he mentioned the bike. A bike! A dream come true! I had to go for an interview that Friday night.

So I made my way to Islington, then a mostly Jewish area with numerous trades-men and small businesses. I went to the back entrance of the given address in a wide back lane. I knocked and was admitted by a very tall bearded man with kind, deep set eyes and skull cap. The first thing I saw was a long table in the yard, heaped high with giblets. I felt sick; although we had kept hens, I had never seen such a quantity of entrails.[3] Mr Ginsberg said my job was to deliver poultry around the city to hotels and boarding houses. He then showed me the bike; it came as some-thing of a shock as it looked as though it had been adapted from a World War One tank. It was enormous, with positions at the back and the front for carrier baskets, kick-down legs so it could stand upright but, oh thankfully, a lady's crossbar. I doubted I would ever have got on the thing with a gent's.

'You can ride it, can't you?' my employer enquired, looking at my startled face.

'Oh yeah, of course!' I lied assuredly, like a would-be actor volunteering for any stunt.

'Be here at seven tomorrow, then,' he said as I left, too overcome by the bike to ask about the wages.

I arrived early next day to meet two women cleaning out yet more chickens. Then I saw the bike and felt faint; stacked high at front and rear with paper covered chickens, it seemed to glare challengingly at me.

'The names of the hotels are on the paper and here's the order list. Good luck, ride carefully,' the boss said as I staggered off. Ride, ride, I could scarcely push the thing as we clattered along the streets. I struggled around the city, visiting the Stork, St George's and the Adelphi on my travels. Eventually the bike was light enough to tackle and I soon became its master, soaring through the busy streets, feeling quite the local hero. I was back at base by two o'clock, in good time for both Harry's and the match.

Mr Ginsberg, or 'I' as everyone called him, seemed pleased.[4]

'Do you go to Mass on Sundays?'

I nodded.

'Go to the first one and then come here; we have more deliveries tomorrow. Oh, take the bike so you can be sure of an early start.'

Take the bike! I was 'made up' as I raced through the streets and deposited it proudly in our back yard. I dashed back on Sunday after Mass, relieved to see there were not as many chickens as the Saturday trade.

The west side of Great Homer Street, looking south from William Moult Street. The post in the centre of the picture outside the corner shop was a fire alarm – you broke the glass and pulled the handle and a bell would ring. We kids had great fun with this! (LIV.R.O.)

'Have you had any breakfast?' the boss asked as I nodded.

'Well, come and have something anyway before you start.'

I went inside the premises and drank tea and had two slices of dark rye bread with 'I' and two of his mates. Then off I rode, determined with some excitement to be as quick as I could, in eager anticipation of my wage packet. I was back by one o'clock, put the bike away and was then given an envelope. I felt upset as it was light and seemed empty.

'Well, aren't you going to open it,' he said, smiling at my disappointed face. I did and, to my delight, found two ten shilling notes, an amazing amount given that some grown men were only bringing home two pounds ten for a full week's work. I stammered my thanks as I left.

'Oh John,' he said finally, 'if you go to your Holy Communion on Sundays, let me know and we will have a big breakfast together.'[5]

Off I went feeling like a man of the world. I entered our house with a certain aplomb and handed over my wages to mother.

'Good God! Two ten bob notes! What's going on? What have you been up to this time?' she shrieked.

'Nothing, mam, honest.'

'The man's mad, he's made a mistake! He's given you the wrong packet! We'll all end up in trouble. Come on, we're going round there.'

Protesting my innocence and the accuracy of the wage, I was still dragged by tram to Islington. 'I' confirmed the amount, as my mother blushed and apologised. Her mood lightened and we got off the return tram at Athol Street where we went into Spenso's and bought some of their delicious lemonade, then to Falavio's, a cross between an Italian fish and chip shop and ice cream parlour. Here again we made luxurious purchases and off home for a party with my brothers. While I gave most of the wages to her, she still lectured about the pocket money I kept.

'Don't spend it all on sweets. Be sensible and put at least three pence a week away in the Post Office,' she exhorted. Wise advice which I never followed.

I worked on the deliveries for some fifteen months and things seemed to improve dramatically at home with my contribution to the meagre family budget. Christmas was great with tips, assorted items from my regulars and a chicken whenever I wanted one. I felt like a millionaire. Harry Silverman always had his fire and gas lit, if not by me then by one of my brothers until we were finally called up for the war.

As Scotland Road got ready for war, I looked forward to leaving school and having a proper job. With the war preparations, the local community seemed to enjoy an economic upturn and things improved on the employment front. Work meant at last being able to wear proper long trousers, garments devoutly to be wished. I left school with an 'excellent character' as the blue card I received from the head was known. Murray also gave me an envelope with a job recommendation which I had to take to the manager of Lunt's cake shop in Latimer Street, next to St Sylvester's school. Sadly full employment meant terminating my delivery job and its perks. I bade a sad farewell to 'I' but looked forward to Lunt's and duly purchased the treasured long trousers and a jacket.

On Monday I reported to the manager, an unpleasant sort who looked like a scowling new pin, well Brylcreemed black hair, spectacles and a dazzling white coat which reached down below his knees, stiff with starch courtesy of our local Chinese laundry. He showed me round into the back of the shop where four lads and a grown man were busy making all kinds of bread, cakes and pastries. They wore sacks for aprons and used sacks to protect their hands as they spent the whole day lifting trays in and out of red hot ovens. The smell was delicious, the heat unbearable.

We went through to the back yard, where another lad was loading box carts with bread. My duties were then explained to me with military precision. A wicker basket was produced, about eighteen inches deep and wide and about two foot long; with some skill the manager showed me how to pack it with twenty-four two pound loaves. It had a sturdy string at the edges which was placed around my neck and I was told to lift it. It was heavy and cut into my skin through my collar. Tissue paper was then stuck down my shirt to stop the rubbing. I was given a list of streets to visit, knocking on doors to sell the loaves. Then came the shock; the wages were six shillings and two pence (31 pence) for a forty-eight hour week. I immediately lost all interest, thinking of the part-time job I had just given up. Noticing my disdain, I was told I could have the princely rise of two shillings after a month's probation. I might also be given a box cart instead of the basket. I kept thinking fondly about 'I' and my old job – and the bike. What a come down!

My first day was no success. I sold three loaves, my neck ached and I was convinced the string would eventually cut off my head. After a couple of hours, I was on the verge of packing it in but I realised there would be all hell to pay at home and respectable jobs were not that plentiful. I managed to increase my sales figures to four on the Tuesday but on the Wednesday the manager gave me a short, sharp rebuke on how to sell. He handed me a new list of streets and insisted I visited each in turn. I was to start two or three miles from the shop in Utting Avenue. Walking downheartedly with the string severing my neck, I decided enough was enough! I never made it to Utting Avenue but sold my usual three loaves and went back to the shop. The manager approached.

'Been to Utting Avenue?' he asked suspiciously.

'Yeah,' I said no longer caring.

'You bloody little liar! I live in Utting Avenue and the wife's just been in and said there was no sign of you.'

'Oh yeah, big deal! Yer jumped up little Hitler! Yer can stick yer job! I'm off.'

Out I stormed, as he proceeded to entertain the rest of the workforce by going quickly berserk. I went home as usual as though nothing had happened and spent a sleepless night worrying about the reaction, not only of my parents but also of Big Murray who had been good enough to recommend me. On the Thursday morning I pretended to set off for work and wandered about aimlessly, deciding one minute to stow away on a ship, then remembering I was as sick as a dog even on the ferry. I tried to concoct ways of seeking my fortune in London.

At this point I was making my way down Bevington Hill when I spotted a provisions warehouse where a man was loading a lorry for 'S. Gordon and Sons'. I thought I had nothing to lose, so I enquired about vacancies. He jumped down from the lorry and said the assistant warehouseman was leaving the next week for the army and to go inside and see a Mr Rooney in a brown overall.

This I did and he took me upstairs to see the owners, a Mr Taylor and son. After a brief interview they asked, to my immense relief, if I could start on Monday. I was over the moon, was duly introduced to Ted who was joining the army and the driver, Bert, who had helped me. They both shook hands and wished me well and I was immediately struck by the warm contrast with Lunt's.

To celebrate, I went round the corner to Thorn's cafe and had the usual soup, roast beef and college pudding. Reality dawned and I counted out my savings; I was one shilling and nine pence short of what my mother would expect on Friday. Old habits die hard and, like a young kid again, I went for a stroll down 'Paddy's Market' and checked the gate in Maddox Street. It was open so I grabbed and bundled together as many clothes as I could carry and went to Packingham's. My lucky day! I got three shillings, enough to satisfy my parents.[6]

I pretended to set off for work again on the Friday and, quite out of character, paid a visit to St Anthony's Church. Here, although never a 'holy Joe', I gave thanks in a mood of great cheer. I returned home at one o'clock and explained to my mother that I had left Lunt's because I was starting a new job on Monday with better pay and prospects.[7] She was genuinely delighted, as was dad who thought I had shown considerable initiative. Lunt's still owe me three days' pay; I could never be bothered to go back and get it.

The following Monday I made my way to my new employ.[8] Mr Rooney turned out to be a very kindly old man. He showed me around the warehouse which seemed piled to the ceiling with food. There was everything you could imagine, half-hundredweight boxes of New Zealand butter, seven pound packets of 'Golden Stream' tea, hundredweights of sugar, jams of all descriptions and tins and tins of salmon, crab and 'Carnation' milk. The list was endless. We then went out into the yard where I was presented with my handcart, low with good springs and big wheels and a damn sight better than the wicker basket. I was to supply the little local grocers. It was 'the gear' going down Bev. Hill; I would sit on the handle and get one wheel against the pavement and practically ride all the way down. I had to push it back up, but I was so happy I did not care.

S. Gordon's had quite a few shops of their own, four alone on Great Homer Street which Bert supplied by lorry. Sometimes I would go with him to help him unload. Trade boomed and I was soon made assistant warehouseman with a ten shilling rise. The war came but all in 'Scottie' seemed better off. I remember going down to Robert's and Bromiley's, the tailors and ordering my first made-to-measure suit with twenty-eight inch trouser bottoms and padded jacket shoulders, then up to Samuel's for a shirt and tie. Two months later, I could afford a made-to-measure overcoat, again with padded shoulders and a fashionable large tie belt.

Now I and the rest of the gang thought we really looked the part; we all had jobs and two had already gone to sea. It was at this point that I realised how times had changed; when I was a child, most men had worn caps, mufflers or scarves; for the fashionable 'salt and pepper' caps had been 'all the go'. Now mufflers and caps were superseded by collars and tie, caps by trilbies and later Stetsons as we began to import our fashion crazes from the States. As a teenager life seemed on the up and up.

So I proceeded, happy in my job from Mondays to Saturday noon, packing orders ready for delivery. Some Saturdays I would go in the boss's car around the shops, collecting the takings which were bagged and given to one of the bosses sitting in the back of the car. All was eventually placed in the warehouse safe until it was banked on Mondays. Rooney could never understand why I was taken on these excursions as he always needed me in the warehouse but we found out later that they were looking further ahead than either of us.

Rooney loved his 'noggin of rum'; he did not carry a flask but always had a flat quarter bottle in his back pocket. As soon as it was empty I would be sent to the pub for a refill although I do not think he was an alcoholic by any stretch of the imagination. He was excellent at his job, knowing every item in the warehouse, where it was and how many needed to be ordered. Once he asked me to his house to help him with the Anderson shelter in the garden.[9] Although he had had it fitted it leaked badly when it rained and he said he had reached the stage when he would rather be bombed than drowned. He had the idea of putting some strong wooden boxes on the floor covered with planks of wood; thus, he reasoned, when it rained it would drain away under this artificial floor. I never found out if this worked.

During the course of the afternoon, he began to talk about his former assistant, Ted, and his call up to the army. He was always pretty annoyed about the whole thing as he said the job was a reserve occupation and thus exempt from military service; he said if I did not want to go, he would ask Mr Taylor, the owner, to write to the Ministry of Labour for my exemption. I then realised how fond he was of me and I of him.

'War proves nothing,' he said with deep bitterness. 'Look at the promises made to servicemen in 1918. None were honoured. Don't go, John, it's not worth fighting when they come to your own front door. Family's important, nothing else counts.'

He never talked about his own World War One experiences but then, as on later occasions, he would brood and get very downhearted, speaking of good mates lost at sea or in France, their lives wasted by incompetence. I began to hate these conversations and worried as he always finished his rum bottle. I would then be sent for some more but always took a long time in the hope he would forget what he had been talking about. Sometimes it worked, sometimes not. Although melancholic but never violent I learned a great deal from him during such chats. I only realised this later, after, in naive, jingoistic innocence, I had joined the army.

Chapter Five

'Boys will be boys!'

From a very early age my friends and I developed the British attitude to work, i.e. you worked to live, to enjoy whatever income came your way. So early jobs around the market and the pennies they provided were essential for our few childhood luxuries and pleasures.

Yet, like most young kids, our best games cost nothing. We had lots of fun climbing, usually backyard walls and then racing along them and jumping across the entry gaps with some daring and skill. As the tops of the 'runs' were only about nine inches wide, we had to be pretty surefooted. Sometimes we fell, usually because of old, decaying brickwork, but it never seemed to discourage us.

Swimming was another cost-free pursuit. In good weather, our favourite spot was the section of the Leeds and Liverpool Canal behind the Tate and Lyle's sugar works in Chisenhale Street. This portion of water was affectionately known as the 'Scaldie', as Tate's discharged very hot liquid into it, no doubt polluting it. Sometimes we honoured Burlington Street free open air baths with our custom.[1] We had to swim for the most part naked and take turns to guard our rags; one day one pal lost all his clothes and had to walk all the way back to 'Bosi', right along Vauxhall Road and up 'Hoppie', with one of our towels preserving his dignity. We laughed all the way, as he delighted in being the star attraction of the streets.

The canals were used by all the local kids; sometimes one would go missing and then a search by local men would ensue. If unsuccessful, the police were informed and when finally Jim Clark arrived, we would fear the worst. He was, beyond doubt, the best underwater swimmer in Liverpool. He would sometimes find a drowned child, trapped by weeds or rubbish tipped by the irresponsible. Despite knowing the risks, we swam undeterred.

Our favourite pastime when pennies allowed was the 'Penny Rip': the latter were bicycles of sorts hired out by Andy Ryan in Kew Street. They had a frame, two wheels and a front or back brake. They cost one penny per hour, although most were past collapse. Nevertheless, we had great fun riding all over Great Homer and between Kew and Wilbraham Streets as it was, for the most part, the only tarmacked road in the area. Real speed was possible but God help you if your 'penny rip' had a front brake; if you had to stop suddenly, you went right over the handlebars with innumerable cuts and bruises. If this happened during term time, your wounds might be spotted and off you would be sent to the clinic in Blackstock Street. Here

The Tate & Lyle works in 1982. These were built around the Leeds and Liverpool Canal basin. On the far left of the picture is where Burlington Cinema was and, behind that, was the free open-air swimming pool.

one suffered the sadistic medical treatment of a local nurse; cuts and grazes were cleaned brusquely with cotton wool and then the dreaded iodine. This, despite earpiercing screams and loud recriminations, was liberally applied and dabbed deep into cuts.[2]

When you are a kid, everything is either an adventure or a challenge. For us visiting the old windmill overlooking 'Scottie' provided both. By 1930 it stood behind McKenna's secondhand furniture shop at the corner of Woodstock Street; it had long lost its sails and had been empty for years. We would scurry to the top and walk around its circular roof to view our majestic city from all angles. It was truly magnificent! We gazed at the Mersey, then alive and bustling with the ships of the world, then looked towards Bootle, picking out the splendour of the 'Rotunda'.[3] Then we studied the hill that led to Netherfield Road, all the streets leading down to Great Homer Street and the masses of people hurriedly going about their business. Finally we would stare out towards Southend, the Pier Head and the Liver Building with its birds, one of the best sights in the world, as Dad often said, for a Scouser coming home from sea.

Up on the roof we once spotted what was to become a regular haunt on rainy days, a disused warehouse at the bottom of Kew Street. It was full of rooms where we could play 'hide and seek' but the main attraction was the lift. It was weighted so one had to pull a rope to the top floor, then let go and have the ride of your life. After many months, the rope snapped and the lift gained uncontrollable speed; thank God we were only on the second floor, as it hit the ground with an almighty thud. We were all very badly shaken and bruised but the only thing that worried us was the thought of the clinic and the infamous iodine.

At about the same time we also came across a quarry which became another play-ground when empty. It stood where the 'Princess Bingo Hall'[4] now stands and manufactured house bricks. On Sundays we would go to the quarry where steel skips were used on railway lines to carry the clay *et al*. We would quickly clear one out if none were already empty and then push it up an incline, all jump in and down we would go, cheering all the way. It was better than the fair and, above all, free. We would stay all day, going home reluctantly as darkness fell.

Darkness always provides opportunities for childhood fun, usually of the frightening, scary variety. We would all sit on the pavement under the gas lamp between the Horans and the Rooneys, telling stories for as long as we were allowed

The Burlington Street bridge over the canal. We used to swim regularly in the canal, though, of course, we were not supposed to! (LIV.R.O.)

out. What added spice to all the proceedings was the ubiquitous street ghost.[5] The Rooney house was supposed to be haunted by a lady in a long dress with black plaited hair; weird tales were also encouraged by the fact that the house itself was quite different to all the others; it had a much broader lobby and a couple of stairs in the lobby leading to the kitchen, although the front parlour was on the street level. There was also a wide staircase leading to the bedrooms, and above the house the gutter had large coping stones adjoining the house next door occupied by the Dicksons. Some people said in the past both homes had been one large property. Word had it that before old Mr Rooney died he was flung off the sofa although the house was empty of all other living souls. The Rooneys themselves gave credence to the ghostly tales, as they moved quickly into the Dicksons' house when they left. As children, we would terrify each other in dark autumn evenings, giggling as we watched grown-ups cross the street rather than pass the house after dusk.

Needless to say, like most little boys, we enjoyed our share of 'giving cheek' and generally harassing adults, especially local tradespeople. We were always being chastised but, as every kid knows, that just adds sparkle to the proceedings and some adults were quite good natured in their verbal discipline. I always remember Mick Daly who had the undertaker's at the corner of Penryhn Street;[6] it had the

The Liver Building can just be seen above the rubble all around Derby Square. The Victoria Monument was about the only structure undamaged in this area after the Blitz. (LIV.R.O.)

The Pier Head buildings seen from the Overhead Railway.

most beautiful stained glass windows in Scotland Road. At the door Mick could often be seen taking the air but, if he went indoors, we would run across, open the door which had a loud, jangling bell and shout, 'Any empty boxes Mick?'

He would shout back, sometimes chuckling,

'Plenty in here, lads, and if you do that again, I'll put you in one!'[7]

During the 1930s, we all loved the summer holidays; here we could travel far and wide, as the Corporation allowed kids to have four rides on their trams for a penny.[8] The tram conductor who took the fares would punch your ticket each time until you had exhausted your quota. Wherever the trams went, so did we; Sefton Park, Aigburth, Garston[9] and the Pier Head. The latter always seems to conjure up memories of the Nestlé's chocolate machines painted bright red. A bar cost a penny but seldom did we all have enough money, so some tried tin bottle tops, mainly from beer bottles, flattened with some skill on the tram lines. Some worked, most didn't. At the Pier Head we often endeavoured to get on a ferry and sneak a free ride to New Brighton. Here, however, the ticket collectors were exceptionally strict. I soon gave up these particular excursions as, although every male member of my family went to sea at some point, I was as sick as a dog, even on a ferry. Things never changed.

When the Mersey tide was out, we could often climb down the chains under the 'floating bridge', catch crabs left behind in the mud and generally get into a terrible mess. Parents were constantly lecturing us about the dangers as well as the washing it created.[10]

Stanley Park was another popular venue; we would walk there to save money

East Scotland Road, Nos 288–318. The old Derby Picture House is on the left. Admission was only a penny on a Saturday, so we all fought to get in during the so-called 'Penny Rush'.

and sometimes, as a great treat, take bottles of water with lemonade powder and stacks of bread and margarine. As always, the added attraction at the park was the open air pool. On sunny days, Seaforth Sands beckoned.[11] Here we played for hours in the sand and slid down a concrete slope, in reality a dyke. You would be exhausted by the climb up the dyke but the slide made it all worthwhile; here we used a seat of either wood or tin, although tin had the disadvantage of getting red hot in the sun, and the friction of sliding causing many a burned bottom. If you came off your wood, then poor trousers would soon suffer and there would be all hell to play at home, with smacks and yet more patches.

I can still remember vividly going to Seaforth with a three by six foot white linen tent, complete with guide ropes, wooden and steel pegs – a prize birthday present bought from Sturlas' in Great Homer Street, no doubt on the 'never-never'. We decided it would be a great adventure to camp out overnight; we took the earliest Number 24 tram, armed with food, towels and tin cans with makeshift wire handles. We struggled to the beach, picked the best spot and proudly pitched the tent. We were the envy of hundreds of other scallywags who only had sack tents. Two of us spent hours looking for drift wood to make our fire which later we lit and proceeded to cook our 'Skilly'; this was a dreadful concoction of all our foodstuffs, potatoes, cabbage, peas and beans, cooked in water without the salt which we regularly forgot. It took hours, was well smoked and generally tasted awful.

The main mistake we made was we never realised how far out the tide got at Seaforth and so our tent was pitched far too close to the incoming water; as darkness fell and the beach slowly emptied, we noticed the ebb and flow of the approaching tide. At first it did not seem too bad; the water only seemed about an inch deep. Then, to our amazement, flash lights and torches appeared. Two policemen began to yell at us.

'What the bloody hell do you think you're up to?'

They then flipped up the tent, pegs and all, and ordered us to follow them. We were herded unceremoniously into a lorry and one policeman travelled in the cab compartment with the driver. We were unloaded back in 'Bosi' when the officer gave our parents the telling off of their lives. This was definitely deliberate, to ensure a good hiding and no repetition of the escapade. By God it worked; the adults,

An electric tram. (LIV.R.O.)

having already spent hours combing the streets for us, were in no mood for excuses; we were all battered black and blue and I never saw the tent again; after that it was back to the sacks and getting home before dark.

Like the beach, the countryside had its share of delights. The Number 22 tram would take us to Fazakerley and then we would walk the rest of the way to Simonswood, then glorious fields and meadows, now Kirkby housing and industrial estate. The last stop on the tram was the 'Reo Cinema' but the trek down Ingoe Lane for kids used to city smog was exhilarating. Again Tate and Lyle sacks and tree twigs provided a makeshift tent. We would spend long summer days catching fish in the Alt and then, dog-tired, make our way home to the tram stop. Sometimes, despite the clatter from the steel wheels on the steel tracks, the ceaseless rattle and stopping and starting, we would even fall asleep on the tram, exhausted but happy.[12] Of course, it had to happen once; we lost our penny returns as we walked down Ingoe Lane in the creeping darkness. A car pulled up and a very posh female voice called out,

'And where are you going at this time of night?'

'Scotland Road, Miss, we've lost our tram tickets so we'll have to walk all the way,' one of us said plaintively, as we all hoped that this touching appeal would result in her giving us our fare.

'Oh get in. It's on my way and it's too dark to walk,' she ordered, to our shock as we tumbled in the back, grinning at our good fortune.

'Sit up straight and if you've got fleas, keep them to yourselves!' she barked.

It was the first time I had ever been in a car, and what a car! It was an American Buick, unbelievable luxury. She drove us back to 'Bosi' and proceeded to give our parents a lecture in roughly the same vein as the Seaforth policeman. It had the same results, a good telling-off and a few well-aimed smacks.

Sometimes we were 'confined to barracks' by having to babysit a much-resented younger brother or sister; again we made the best of summer days if we could lay our hands on an old lorry tyre.[13] If successful, we would take it and our charges to Aughton Street, famous among local kids for its inclines, and then take it in turns to get inside the tyre, helped by the others. One would hold it upright while another kept an eye on the traffic situation. The idea was to compete for the longest roll. It took quite a while to overcome the pleasant giddiness. When we had finished we often gave the tyre to anyone who wanted it. Playing around in the streets, albeit under duress, could result in a little extra income, as adults regularly asked children to 'go on messages' and occasionally rewarded them for doing so.

As we grew older, football, both the playing and the supporting, took up an increasing amount of our time, popularised perhaps by the growing success of both local teams. We found we could go to the match at three-quarter time, free of charge, as the officials opened the gates to avoid a last minute crush to the exits. In the 1930s Everton was the more successful but, strangely for a Catholic then, I became a committed Liverpool supporter.[14]

Real interest in younger lads was created by the Catholic Schools Football League; you always supported your own school but I think, to be fair, St Sylvester's had the best team for most of the 'thirties. One team that always stuck in our young, impressionable minds was that of St Edward's Orphanage. The lads made a great side and attracted large crowds whenever they played at either Liverpool's or Everton's ground. They seemed huge, like grown men, but this was probably because of their regular orphanage diet and hard training. We all pitied their orphan status and even slipped them coppers before they were marched back to the home. It was almost like warding off bad luck as we all dreaded being orphans. In reality we knew little or nothing about such places except that the discipline was harsh. Enough said! There were rumours that the boys were eventually settled on work in Canada. For this reason, in every street there were girls who would take on very early maternal responsibilities and often thus relinquished their own chances of marriage to avoid younger brothers and sisters being sent to institutions such as St Edward's.[15]

Not all our pastimes were out of doors; our hard-earned pennies were regularly spent going to the picture houses, especially the crazy 'Penny Rush' at the Derby Cinema on Saturdays. This was an experience not to be missed, as what seemed like thousands of children were herded like cattle down a narrow passage on the right-hand side of the picture house; the further down the passage you went, the narrower it got until eventually you reached the cinema door where an usherette would take your ticket, if it had survived the journey.

Once inside, you would do your best to sit with your mates; some of the seats were no more than long planks of wood, so when one kid stood up all the rest were affected. There was always pandemonium, noise reaching all time levels during a good picture. We reserved a special outcry for the fireman', a bloke who would walk up and down the aisles once everyone was seated spraying the air with a pump full of disinfectant. Sometimes there was a technical hitch and we all roared as we were showered with chemicals. Imagine anything like that today!

The area abounded, as in every built-up community, with cinemas. Scotland Road alone had two, the Derby and the Gaiety.'[16] Further afield, there were the Gem, Burly, Homer, Rossi, Tivoli, Popular, 'Grovie' and the Garrick, to name but a few. We even had two great theatres, the Rotunda between Scotland Road and Stanley Road and the Lyric at the bottom of Everton Valley. I never went to the Lyric to see a show, although we did play inside it before it was demolished. In the good old Rotunda we spent many happy hours, paying threepence to sit in the 'gods' as the highest seats were called. The foyer gave us a glimpse of real wealth as the elite of Liverpool's outskirts arrived, increasingly by car, dressed in their finery, gentlemen in top hats and ladies in long evening gowns. The foyer seemed the epitome of elegance, with fine carpets and statues of beautiful women holding electric lamps. Needless to say the immaculately tailored doormen always tried to chase us ragged kids away until our betters had entered.

Yet even the theatres had their share of Scouse legends. Before the war, a very small, shawled woman called Mary Blunn fluctuated between the Rotunda and the Great Homer cinema selling fruit from a large wicker basket. Most was good but we always bought the cheapest 'fades', at tuppence a go. She became part of the local landscape to such an extent that I was told by several people that Lord Haw-Haw had said the German air force were going to raze Liverpool to the ground, including Mary Blunn.'[17] This caused consternation and served to strengthen the resolve of the community against Hitler!

Thus in youth and teenage years before we began to indulge in more adult pursuits of pubs and dance halls, Scotland Road in particular and Liverpool in general teemed with areas of play and amusement. Like most of my generation I often view with pity and sympathy the kids of the late twentieth century who seem lost at play and who spend hours in front of the telly or video. They've no idea what they're missing!

Chapter Six

Life for the grown-ups

As a young child, I always remember being surprised at the many ways adults tried to earn money during the hard times. 'Rag tattering' was a common trade, the rag tatters exchanging money, balloons, goldfish or even little live chicks for rags. Some people managed to rear the chicks successfully and reaped the rewards of regular eggs and a potential Christmas dinner. One man tried to make some kind of living by offering to sharpen knives, scissors *et al* on a grind stone which he wheeled around the streets. One Jewish bloke carried a large canvas bag strapped across his shoulders; inside he kept glass and he would knock on doors asking to repair cracked windows. One man regularly appeared with a handcart full of blocks of salt, about two foot by eight inches square; he would cut off slices with a handsaw, the size depending on what you were prepared to pay.

Selling ice cream was another job some tried, using three-wheeler bikes which had boxes attached containing ice to keep the produce cool. Then the Italians came on the scene with their handcarts full of white ice cream in a kind of lidded bucket packed on all sides with ice. We thought it was delicious, though the best was 'Gonella's'. One enterprising character had a horse-drawn merry-go-round; he attracted kids wherever he stopped, charging a ha'penny a ride, rising to a penny if demand sufficed. He had to turn a large handle to work the device; it always looked really hard work keeping the ride going. As ever, street singers and buskers were a common sight.

Women seemed to be at the sharpest end of the labour market; a lot undertook cleaning jobs to make ends meet. Among the most disadvantaged were the ship cleaners, nearly always very poor women with large families. When one of the big ships docked, you would see the women in their shawls, carrying buckets and scrubbing brushes, scurrying down to the dock. Not all would be taken on and a regular, demoralising sight was the return of the unhired.

Casual labour was the curse of many an adult's life in the 1930s. Certain large firms were notorious for hiring men at random; the men would gather like fodder from 7 a.m. onwards and would be given work as and when it suited the employer. The work was hard and shabbily paid but all knew that there was no room for complaint, the answer to which was instant dismissal. Some men were so desperate for work that they would offer to do extra unpaid tasks such as cleaning the boss's house or doing his garden. One firm practised this type of economic apartheid until the mid 1950s and there are always those who would like to see it reintroduced today.

The north side of Benledi Street. Just off the picture, to the right, was James O'Hare's pawnshop.

The minds of adults and kids alike in the early 1930s seemed preoccupied with one single, all-consuming subject, food. Great Homer Street abounded with horse and carts loaded with all kinds of vegetables brought into the city from outlying rural areas like Scarisbrick, Lydiate, Maghull and Aintree. Their destination might be the market in Great Nelson Street. When times were at their toughest, we kids might quickly try to jump on a cart and throw what veg we could grab to our mates down below in the street. None of it was ever wasted but taken home for cooking. 'Salt fish' was a favourite with the adults for Sunday breakfast. It was bought on a Saturday night and steeped in water overnight. We used to get ours from Rooney's in Scotland Road; on Sundays straight after Mass, people would pour out of St Anthony's and across to Rooney's for fruit and veg.

We boys often took the chance after Mass to go 'fishing' with a very thin steel latt about eight feet and an inch and a half wide, usually acquired from the mattress of an old bed. We would bend the end over about two inches at right angles and then set out seeking our fortune.

Most shops and all the pubs along Scottie and Great Homer had cellars for their deliveries, covered by cast iron grids. The latter were about four foot by three with inch slots to let in the daylight. We would place the latt through one of the slots and if it reached the bottom, start 'fishing' for any copper or silver coins dropped by passers-by during the week. Success depended on steady nerves as the latt would shake. We later improved our chances when we started to use a long cane with a tablespoon attached to it, the spoon's front being flattened first. We were never able to spend too long on all this as we would be summoned home for the salt fish breakfast. I loved it smothered in margarine; otherwise it was fairly tasteless.

The shops in Great Homer would stay open very late in the evenings; on Saturdays some might still be open at midnight. Many had stalls outside the shop fronts, laden with all kinds of meat and ribs. Not all had ice lockers and we soon found those with no cooling systems; sometimes when it was very late these shopkeepers would give us the meats they thought would not keep.

One shopkeeper who was very kind to us as kids was the German pork butcher between Newsham Street and St Anthony's Place; he was quite an elderly man, but I remember he once gave us a lot of German sausage and some marvellous salmon cream. The latter was in a large glass bowl; all he asked was that we returned the bowl on Monday morning. By God, I was outside at 8.30 a.m. with one spotless bowl.

A demolished court near Scotland Road West. (LIV.R.O.)

Scotland Road Rotunda Junction, complete with traction engine, in 1904. The only thing which is left is the gents' toilet, now unused and minus the globe on top! (LIV.R.O.)

As we grew older, when we had a few pennies, we came to use the local canteens or 'cannie houses'. One across from the market in Great Nelson Street was Ma Masons', run by Maggie Dyer. She was very kind and if any one of the gang had no money she would still give them a cup of tea and some toast, presumably paid for from her own pocket. She lived in Kew Street and later in life I came to know her well and spent many a happy hour laughing about bygone days.

When we left Maggie's, we would stroll along Great Homer, first stopping at Woolworths. Nothing was more than sixpence and I always remember the cups at sixpence and the saucers at three; they seemed really good quality as very cheap white ones could be bought almost anywhere. The spectacle counter fascinated us; it would be heaped high with all kinds of 'specs' and there was always a crowd around it searching for the right pair; some people took hours trying on between twenty and thirty pairs before they found some that suited. The frames were again sixpence and the lens threepence each.

Next door to Woolworths was Jackson's the hairdressers. It was very unusual in that it was in a cellar and had two lady barbers as well as one man. They were very friendly people and would always give children sweets, usually barley sugars, when they were cutting their hair. I later found out that they were brother and sisters, Leslie, Ada and Hilda. None had married. I was saddened years after when the last time I spoke to them they were all in their eighties and one sister had lost her sight. The old cellar, their life blood, had by this time been filled in with concrete and they lived behind in a flat; still in faded paint on the wall was the sign 'Jackson's Hairdressers, 92 Great Homer Street'. It seemed such a pathetic end for three people with 250 years' service between them to the local community.

Sometimes, funds permitting, we would bypass Woolworths and make our way to the Poplar Cinema in Netherfield Road. I hated the walk up the hill. When we came out of the 'Pop', we would often stop to play in Havelock Street which must have been the steepest in Liverpool; down both sides there were railings to help people; the pavements were also special as they were filled with holes and we assumed that this was to get a better grip in snow or ice. Cast iron bollards closed the street to horses and carts but I never understood how people managed to live there; they must have had the best leg muscles in the city. I often used to wonder how the public services like ambulances and fire engines could do their job and whiled away many a moment pondering how the funeral hearses coped.

If we did not fancy moving so far afield, Bosi had its own 'cookhouse' in the form

Scotland Road in 1908, showing Crane's premises at the junction of Hornby Street. An unpopular eight-hour shift for the policemen consisted of point duty directing the traffic and the trams so that they did not collide with each other.

of Mrs Boardman's terraced house. She was renowned for her cooking and her son, Dickie, a joiner by trade, built a flap across her lobby which served as a counter. Here we would queue up when we could afford it for soup, rice and all kinds of snacks. Prices started at a penny but you always got your money's worth.

Later we discovered Thorn's cannie house in Scotland Road itself and then we fluctuated between it and Mrs Boardman's. You were always guaranteed a laugh in Thorn's listening to Aggie continually yelling down the food chute. The main meal was usually lentil soup, roast beef sandwiches and college pudding. They always opened very early to cater for the market people in Paddy's Market opposite the shop and the fruit market in Great Nelson Street.

Great Nelson Street fruit market provided the most frightening experience of my childhood. It had several entrances but the one on the left hand side of Great Nelson Street itself had a big square behind it, about eight foot by ten sealed off by two large six foot high wooden gates. The traders used this square to dump faded fruit and it used to be full in a couple of days; it was then emptied by binmen who opened a small insert gate in the main ones and shovelled all the 'fades' into their carts. The market police or 'keepers' were always chasing us away from this spot. As not all

Latimer Street in 1934. This is the street where I started work in Lunt's Cake Shop. (LIV.R.O.)

Another view of part of Latimer Street in the 1930s. (LIV.R.O.)

the fruit was bad, we used to take it in turns to sit on the top of the gates and pick off the good stuff.

One fateful day it was my turn; I was stretching over to grab some reasonable looking apples when one of the mates yelled 'Keeper!' and I lost my grip and fell into a sea of faded fruit. It was terrifying; I began to sink, I could not find anything to grab; every time I screamed and struggled, I sank deeper and deeper, panicking for breath amongst the rotten, decaying pulp. By the time my head was covered, it had been an eternity. Then suddenly the whole side of the square just seemed to collapse and I rushed out headlong with all the fruit. As luck would have it, my mate had told the keeper who promptly unlocked the gates. (They all carried their keys as a symbol of authority.) Two men picked me up out of the mess and asked if I was hurt. 'No,' came the answer and so they chased me for all the trouble I had caused. Then came the Scouse humour as my mates walked me home. The comments were quick and fast, the smell disgusting. So many people asked what was wrong with me, that one pal, exasperated, stated bluntly,

'He's just fell down a shithouse, what do yer think!'

A painting of Great Homer Street between Virgil Street and Rachel Street in 1886. (LIV.R.O.)

There was hell to pay when I got home; despite years of experience in a house full of lads, my mother looked visibly shocked at my state.

'What 'ave yer been up to now?'

'Oh, just playin'.'

Out came the big galvanised bath from its spot in the backyard. The contents of the old cast iron kettle was emptied in it and within the hour I was clean and out in the street playing football, none the worse for the exploit.

The street was not the exclusive preserve of the young. Adults, too, played their own games, much to our amusement. On Saturdays and Sundays, on the hollow facing the mission hall there was a regular 'Toss School'. Men would gather and the school would be run by three or four men, one as the 'belt man', another the moneyholder and bet payer and the others as lookouts or 'dowzees'. The latter kept an eye out for the police as such pastimes were illegal. Anyone could toss the two ha'pennies but they first had to put so much money with the moneyholder; it could be anything from two pounds upwards. The moneyholder would then take the bets from anyone in the crowd, usually from sixpence upwards until he had enough to cover the two pounds stake. People would then bet that the two coins would come down 'tails up' or 'the Brittania side'; if they landed 'heads up' the tosser won. Then the moneyholder would call for more bets to cover the four pound stake. If the coins came down showing one head and one tail, then the tosser kept throwing until both sides were the same and gave a result. The tosser could throw for as long as he liked or if, after showing 'heads up' on four throws, he could retire with his winnings, having paid the belt man and the others their commission. The strict rule of the game was that the tosser always had to throw the coins above his head; if he did not, any member of the toss school could shout 'Bar them!' and the coins would have to be rethrown. On occasions, this led to fierce arguments among the men; the belt man now came into his own and settled the trouble with his fists.

Most belt men were tough guys or 'hard knocks' and generally got their own way. Sometimes the fight would be settled later with the protagonists challenging each other to a fist fight on the 'lockfields', i.e. some waste land alongside the canal at the bottom of Lightbody Street. These fights could last a good while with the contestants battering each other with bare fists but, when honour was satisfied, the men, as usual, became friends for life or at least until the next fight.

The police did all in their power to outwit the 'dowzees', no easy job in Liverpool,

Great Homer Street, looking north from Newsham Street. The building with the stone façade is where the Great Homer Cinema was. Mary Blunn sold fruit on the left-hand door. (LIV.R.O.)

The Hamlet pub at the corner of Boundary Street and Kirkdale Road. All the houses alongside were doctors or dentists in the 1930s. They are all boarded up now.

and put an end to the 'toss schools'. Sometimes they would sneak down entries and back lanes in plain clothes, pretending to be locals in the hope of getting close enough to the 'school' to nab a few miscreants.

The police never had a great success rate, as neighbours would always help the players. As far as the latter were concerned, the men were doing no real harm. Thus it became standard practice to leave backyard doors open so that players could run in during a raid. It all seemed quite normal for us as children to be sitting down for a meal when a man would dash in, throw off his cap and coat, quickly grab a chair and make himself at home. If the police followed, which they never did, all were prepared to swear the bloke had been in the house for, oh, at least an hour.

Having said that, front doors seemed permanently left open until late at night, there being a strict local rule that you never stole from your own kind. Thus adults would leave string hanging through letter boxes all night so they could open their doors by pulling the string and without disturbing anyone.

Gambling was an adult hobby, as indeed was drinking, which still remains the easiest way to forget sorrows and the pressure of poverty. For a short time the 'mission hall' in 'Bosi' became a club for men only, with a bouncer on the door; later it involved card playing for money. Then the police found out. The day they raided it went down in local folklore; some twenty to thirty officers surrounded the building, some with axes and down the street came the 'Black Maria' as we called the police van. They hammered at the door and were refused entry. Then the axes went to work on the heavy oak doors; meanwhile men were furtively escaping through the fanlight onto the roof. The crowd watched in absolute silence but then

Left The Corner House, a pub on the corner of Athol Street. Lower down Athol Street on the other side was the local police station.

Below left This pub on the corner of Hopwood Street was known as the Blackpool House in the 1930s.

Below right At the corner of Boundary Street and Scotland Road was another pub by the name of 'Hamlet'. This one was owned by Walkers, the other by Whitbreads.

an officer spotted them; quite a lot got away but a few were caught and shoved into the 'Maria' as the people cheered and applauded the culprits. They were then taken to either Athol Street or Rose Hill police stations and later to court to be fined.[1]

Not that the community disliked the police; indeed the opposite was true. Three local 'bobbies' were known affectionately by their nicknames, 'Buck', 'Old Nick' and 'Three Ones' (i.e. 111D). They along with Sergeant McNaughton, were respected by most people for the fair way they carried out their duties.

We kids were naturally always up to mischief, skipping rides on lorries, jumping on the back bumpers of trams or playing football where it was forbidden. If any one of them caught us we would get a clip round the ear and a telling off. Parents would always be informed and that meant a hiding and bed. These particular policemen were so well liked by the adults that they were often asked to weddings and Christmas parties. Then they really joined in the fun but we never took advantage of their friendship, nor they of ours.

Some policemen were, however, loathed for their arrogance; two were stationed at Rose Hill station and were nicknamed the 'Botany Bay Jacks'. They hated the local people, openly referring to them as 'trash' and 'vermin'. They always did their best to get people to court for any minor misdemeanour. I well remember when we accidentally broke a window playing rounders. Later both 'Jacks' paid us all a call to state that we were being taken to court. We had already had a collection for a replacement window! When the lady with the broken window found out, she was very upset and insisted upon accompanying us to the court. She went in first and spoke to a clerk, we never had to go into the actual courtroom and that was the last we heard of our heinous crime.

The pubs were the obvious centres for adult enjoyment; by their very lay-out they were the height of local class consciousness. The bars were for the 'riff raff', real 'spit and sawdust' rooms, while the parlours or 'lounges' were resplendent with highly polished tables, chairs, polished floors and even carpets in some. For such luxuries, the clientele had to pay a penny extra on their pints, other drinks pro-rata. Pub managers personified the class distinction of the age, with their white collar, tie, waistcoat and their badge of office, a gold watch with chain hung across the waistcoat pockets. At closing time out came the watch in full view of all the customers. The time would be slowly studied and compared to that of the big clock on the wall. Then came the authoritative shout of 'Time please!' If this had to be repeated, the manager's language would, by subtle gradations, degenerate to foul abuse. Finally some customers might be 'barred out'; no reason had to be given for such a ban and the same is true today.

In the late 1920s, a firm called 'Ind Coope and Allsops' put the cat among the pigeons by refurbishing their bars with coloured lino, cushion chairs and polished tables, at no extra cost to the customers. They thus attracted a very good trade so that other firms reluctantly had to follow suit.

The pubs attracted the seafaring fraternity, a unifying factor being a common fondness for liquor but they added local colour with their reminiscences and debates. Often the trick question would come up about the number of pubs in Scotland Road;

there were a staggering fifty in all, not counting those on the street corners with their addresses down the side streets.

Some men would boast about pub crawling Scottie Road without getting drunk. I never thought this possible and was always very sceptical of such claims. Imagine even if you just had a gill[2] in all of these, you would be legless! The strength of pre-war beer also needs to be considered in such flamboyant bravado. A common habit however, was, to have a 'couple of wines'[3] in Yates' Wine Lodge, followed by a couple of pints on the way home up Scottie; it was, until relatively recently, a cheap way of getting sloshed.

The pubs could also provide entertainment when allowed; officially you could not sing in a pub before the war, although people always did. The police, always a sergeant and a constable, paid regular visits to stop the noise. As long as everyone stopped as soon as they entered, there would be no real trouble but if some idiot tried to be clever and carry on singing, he would make life very awkward for the manager. Thus if he was arrested, he was guaranteed to be 'barred out' in the future. After the war, the rules were relaxed; perhaps we had proven ourselves and four pubs were granted music licences and acquired pianos.[4]

Generally the adult world is largely an irrelevance to a young child but almost imperceptively we began to develop the sort of sexual stereotyping, later to be the bane of modern feminism. The man in Scotland Road had to be 'macho', tough and dominant in his relationships with women and children. As a young boy the worst term of derision was, thus, 'cissie', a generalisation used to describe any form of behaviour seen as unmanly, for example carrying a comb or an umbrella or, even worse, passing the 'scholarship' and wearing a college blazer. I well remember burning with humiliation when I was catcalled thus for pushing my brother in his pram. I later felt that this crazy desire to be a tough guy ruined many a decent relationship between man and wife, although the women, for the main part, seemed to accept it, at least in public.

Then as now, if truth be known, most working-class families tended to be private matriarchies. Yet 'Scottie' had its share of nascent feminists; two women in particular refused to put up with such nonsense, much to the scandalised amusement of the others. There was one 'hard case' who always boasted about 'being the boss' and not tolerating any 'back chat' in his house. Then one infamous Sunday lunchtime, he was sitting in the pub giving the other men the benefit of his Victorian authoritarianism when in walked his wife, plus pram and two children. In her hands was a plate with his Sunday dinner! She placed it on the bar and turned to the assembled mass.

The kids are waiting for yer to take them the park. I can't. I'm off to me mam's to see if she's better.

I expect that he never lived it down.

The front entrance of Penhryn Street
Church of England School.

St Anthony's priest's house with the
church in the background. The fore-
ground was one of our playgrounds in the
1930s.

Social values plus his seafaring put a sad distance between my father, George, and his sons. I only got to know him much later in life and then there was not much time left. Some memories do still linger; I think we all loved him dearly. It always seemed better when he was home but it did have its drawbacks. We dreaded him being home in the winter. He would get us up for school every morning, shouting with a perverse humour.

'Come on, get up! The sun's crackin' the flags.'

He would then march all of us into the back yard and we would have to wash, one by one, under the cold water tap. When he was away, my mother heated the big cast iron kettle with hot water and we washed in a bowl in the kitchen. Oh, the luxury! He had obviously picked up such discipline in the Royal Navy which he had joined as a young lad to escape a hated stepfather. Like most servicemen, his own personal appearance was immaculate; he seemed to have the same brown suit for years but when he went out, the creases in his trousers were like razor blades and his brown shoes sparkled. Mostly he would only be going for a walk or the odd pint.

On Saturday nights we would be allowed to wait up for him as he always brought some sweets home, usually 'Creamy Whirls', brown and white toffees bought from Meeson's near Paddy's Market. Thus, through his strictness his kindness shone.

Christmas was always special when he was home; there seemed to be plenty to eat and even presents; in addition to the usual apple and orange, there might be new clothes and books. One Christmas stands out in stark contrast to normal, that of 1936; when we got up there were three bikes in the parlour, one for each of us, the 24-inch wheel was mine and the 26-inchers were for the brothers. They were obviously not new but Dad had bought them second-hand and had all but rebuilt them and added a final lick of paint. To us they were veritable Rolls Royces, though how he hid them from us I never found out. Most parents made their kids' presents for Christmas and birthdays; poverty was definitely the mother of invention. When Dad came home again in the late spring, he too got a bike and took us all to Simonswood with sandwiches and lemonade. God, it was some ride, with Dad protecting our rear on our 'bone rattlers'. By the time we got home, we actually volunteered to go to bed.

The women's lives were rarely of interest to young lads. We all knew when mother was going to have another baby but only on the actual day did it really affect the normal day-to-day routine. Then a couple of neighbours would arrive and one of us would have the day off school. It was my turn in 1932; I had to make sure, like in the cowboy films, that there was plenty of hot water. I was relegated to the kitchen to give it a good clean. I remember one attendant getting me to fetch the 'Zebo' blacklead polish.

'Right, get crackin' on the hob, oven and surround!'

What a job! As the fire was lit, the sweat poured off me. I did not really think what was going on with mother, I was too full of my own misery. Then back came the neighbour.

'Not bad, not bad! But yer forgot the kettle.'

After that I remember thinking that life was pretty lousy for women with big families. On balance they were probably a tougher breed than most of the men.

There was one major divisive force among the adult community; Liverpool with its mixed Irish population had, a century earlier, inherited religious bitterness. It bred unrestrained amid poverty and ignorance. The heights of bigotry achieved by some Catholics and Anglicans were veritable Everests, particularly in the Scotland Road and Netherfield Road communities. The former was predominantly Catholic, the latter C of E, the 'border' being Great Homer Street. Religious festivals were always potential flashpoints but 17 March and 12 July, were always the most provocative. On St Patrick's Day the Catholics used to march with their bands and flags. This tended to die out but the wearing of shamrock could still cause trouble. Nowadays even this is far more muted, no doubt because of the 'troubles' in Northern Ireland since the late 'sixties.

The 12 July was a spectacle both to behold and to despair. On the day before, barriers were erected along Great Homer in preparation for the Orange marches. On the morning of the 12th itself the police would be posted in front of the barriers as the various lodge bands assembled. They would come from all over Liverpool, down Everton Valley, along Great Homer Street, all the time being joined by local lodges. Sometimes it would take an hour or more for all to pass the bottom of 'Bosi'. Here I watched, the first time being deafened by the noise. There were hundreds of people, sashes, instruments, drums of all shapes and sizes, even bagpipes, but the catcalls and abuse from both sides of the religious divide were terrible. Given the venom, I was amazed to think that half of the lodge members were on their way to day out in New Brighton. Worse was yet to come when the lodges came home at six or seven o'clock. By then, alcohol had had its usual effects on both groups and the poisonous abuse would pour out. A good many people chose not to watch this evening mayhem.

One thing I never understood was why the Roman Catholic Archbishop, Dr D. Downey and the leader of the Orange Lodge, Rev. Longbottom, never publicly condemned this behaviour. Religion and politics, then as now, are beyond common sense. In some ways it was a great shame as all the processions could have been great events as the people involved looked their best but, sadly, Liverpool missed yet another boat.

One comic note was added, however, by the antics of 'Irish Mary', who lived in

York Terrace; she was of indeterminate Irish descent and annually celebrated both the 17th and the 12th. She would don a hat and shawl and totter to the pub on her wooden leg like a female Long John Silver. Once installed in the alehouse, she would get out of her mind on drink and everyone would keep their distance. Then out came her old, battered holdall and she would pull out an old World War One steel bayonet. She would swing it about blindly shouting crazed abuse. One 17th, she got her wooden leg stuck down a grid outside Joe Allen's pub. Eventually the police arrived with the ubiquitous 'Black Maria'. God, what a job they had to drag her and the grid into the van! She was taken to Athol Street police station to dry out; the grid was returned within the hour.

The funny thing about all this religious bitterness was that, although I went to St Anthony's, half of my mates were C of E and attended Penryhn Street or Roscommon Street schools. St Anthony's had a Young Catholic Men's Society who met in the cellar to play billiards but nothing for the younger kids. Penryhn Street, however, had a play centre two nights a week, here you could play football on the roof covered by wire mesh to keep in the ball or box in the gym in the basement. All the classrooms seemed to be full of activities. I decided to gatecrash with some Protestant pals one night but they briefed me as to what class and teacher I belonged. Lo and behold, we were quizzed by a member of staff but I got in despite a slight mistake. Down in the gym the teacher began to train a crowd of us in boxing, taking the lads in turn to box with the gloves, pointing out faults and giving corrections. Then he picked on me; I was shocked at his choice of partner. It was like David and Goliath but I 'went down fighting', with a black eye and a cut lip. This only served to encourage me and back I went next week. The teacher kept me back and after the 'rush' had gone in, he said very quietly, 'If your parish priest finds out you have been coming here, I will be in serious trouble.'

'Well, I won't tell him if you don't.' I replied. He roared with laughter and I went regularly for many months.

It is difficult nowadays to describe the power a parish priest had over his flock. Ours was a Father Sharkey; a stricter man you could not meet. He was feared by everyone in the parish, most adults regularly displaying blind deference in every encounter with him. His greatest weapon was his calling; his second, his education. In the midst of illiteracy and ignorance, his words would destroy any who dared to challenge his authority or his opinions. I well remember him attending one of our lessons and asking if anyone had any questions on religion. One brave soul asked a particularly tricky query and was told with immediate firmness that the topic was 'one of the seven Blessed Mysteries' which required no explanation but unquestioning faith. I later found out that this was a standard reply used by many clerics when faced with a delicate theological point.

Father Sharkey had several curates to assist him, priests being more plentiful then than now. I remember Fathers Coughlin, Duffy, O'Keefe and Clarkson. After Mass on Sundays one of the curates along with a member of the Catholic Young Men's Society would visit local houses for the weekend collection. The CYMS member would give a loud knock on the door and shout the priest's name to give the family some warning. There would then be a panic and scramble for some coppers. Even in the heights of the depression, people never complained about such collections and would never refuse a priest money. As times improved the priests were streetwise enough to change collection night to Fridays when most had been paid. There were a few of us healthy sceptics who resented the priests' powers particularly in hard times. One mate summed it up thus; 'I can't understand our religion. Our Lord went round on a donkey but just look at Father Sharkey's house and his lovely car. He's always askin' for money! Our Lord didn't.'

We had regular collections in school for the 'waifs and strays', not that we had much to give. We always thought that this bunch had to be in a really bad way if they had to ask the likes of us for help, the only difference we could see was that they were black, we were white.

If some of us were later to look back on the religion of our childhoods with a tinge of resentment, the same religion also provided vivid memories of good times. One of the best years of my childhood was 1933; the big event was St Anthony's centenary. The local Catholics bedecked the streets with glorious bunting; they even made lattice woodwork for round their windows and doors which were then decorated with flowers made of crepe paper. At the top of the street between the two pubs, a large archway was erected, again saturated in paper flowers. The over-all effect was sheer magnificence. People came from all over Liverpool to admire our efforts. The decorations stayed up for a week and when they came down, the old street never looked quite the same.

Religion also provides landmarks in a youngster's life. Every now and again it gave you an opportunity to feel important. My first Communion was one obvious event; next came my Confirmation. We were informed by our teachers, with great solemnity, that the Archbishop himself would be coming to St Anthony's to give us this sacrament and we all had to have a 'guardian' to stand for us at the service. I asked John Loftus, the local 'bookie',[5] to be mine. Having acquired a guardian, the next excitement was choosing a name; we picked all kinds of names, only to be told that they were all against the rules; it had to be a saint's name, a group of illustrious individuals with whom we had very little in common. Eventually the gang made its usual collective decision; we were all to be Joseph, God knows why! We inquired from our elders and betters as to what happened at the actual ceremony. We were told that the Archbishop gave you a real good smack to see if you were tough enough and, if you did not cry, you got your new name. We began to feel distinctly uneasy. It was all a load of bunkum and people were just pulling our legs. The Archbishop just walked along a whole line of us, gently stroking our cheeks and muttering in Latin. After this, it was back to the big attraction, the party. I was even more fortunate in that my guardian gave me half-a-crown (twelve and a half pence), a princely sum.

Just as religion was a divisive force, so football proved to be a source of healthy unification. While both Everton and Liverpool were given religious affiliations, the former Catholic, the latter Protestant, it was more in humour than in hatred. To me public interest seemed to start in the early 1930s. As kids, we took it in turns to go to both grounds at three-quarter time when the officials would open the gates, ready to let the crowd out; we would dash in and see about twenty minutes of play for nothing. Football support became an addiction for many and so remains. Despite my religion I supported Liverpool though it caused 'some stick' at school and, to be fair, in the 'thirties, Everton was the better team.

So, just as St Anthony's centenary was an 'event', Everton's victory in the 1933 FA Cup provided yet another spectacle. Scotland Road was packed but we had a really good spot to watch the team come home. Joe Allen, the manager of a local pub, allowed us kids to watch from one of the windows above his pub. We even had cake and lemonade while we waited for the open landau with Dixie Dean to pass. Years later I won many bets as I used to say I was in a pub and someone would always rise to the bait and dispute my age.

I earnestly believe that Liverpool and Everton were the best thing that ever happened to break down barriers in our community. Even the geographical positions of the grounds helped, as people had to walk up the Valley together; this encouraged conversations, not only about football but many other topics. Then came the singing, sometimes religious, mostly witty.

On a more personal note, the best footballer I ever knew lived in our street, Chris Woodfall. All his family were staunch Evertonians and Chris was brilliant with any type of ball, paper, tennis or 'casey'. You name it, he could do it, dribble, shoot etcetera, etcetera. Every time we picked sides, I knew that if Chris was on our side we would win. We all said he should have been in a proper team but it was not to be; he had a deformed leg which was shorter than the other. My heart used to bleed for him as he was a born natural. Later in life, even with children a lot younger than himself wherever there was a ball, Chris would be playing.

Sport in general brought people together and this was accentuated by the dawn of radio. My father bought one of the old battery wirelesses, a 'Cossor', which worked on an enormous battery and accumulator; the latter was a glass jar containing metal plates. It had to be topped up with acid and recharged at least every ten days. We always took ours to Bennett's in William Moult Street. Wirelesses encouraged knowledge and discussion and even prodded some to learn more by joining the local library at the corner of Collingwood Street.[6] I remember hearing my first Grand National on our wireless in the parlour; the window was opened to let neighbours listen. 'Golden Miller' was the winner.

The National itself provided yet another exciting annual event. A good many people looked forward to 'Jump Sunday' i.e. the Sunday before the race when the course was open to the public to walk around and examine the fences. We would walk all the way to Aintree, sometimes only to be sent packing as we had arrived too late.

The National, in late March or April, reminded us that it would not be long before the Cart Horse Processions in May. Farmers, firms, carters and private individuals used to compete for the best turned out horse, with brasses shining and tails plaited and adorned with flowers. They seemed to take hours passing along Great Homer Street to assemble in the North Market in Great Nelson Street before heading towards town, the Old Haymarket and the final judging. Before moving off the farmers would get rid of any food they did not want; sometimes we would end up with lots of sandwiches and fruit.

Thus we were gradually, almost unconsciously, eased into the adult world by common interests in sport and entertainment. Conversations with adults became more frequent, detailed and articulate. Without realising it, you had slipped through and out of childhood into their and now your world.

Chapter Seven

Getting ready for 'Gerry'!

In 1939 life took on a noticeable change. I was gearing up for the world of full-time work and anxious to finish school, when my father came home from sea for good. My brothers and I found out later that he was very ill but, at the time, he spared us the worry by saying he decided we needed him on a more permanent basis. He added that after twenty-two years of seafaring, ten in the Royal Navy and twelve in the Merchant Navy, he was fed up and wanted a shore job.

This proved to be no easy matter. He got a casual job as a second man on a lorry but never knew when he would be required nor how much he would earn by the end of the week. Eventually, as war approached, he got a permanent job as a boilerman in a factory. He then seemed a lot happier.

During this time we grew to know him. One weekend he took my second eldest brother and myself on a trip on the Overhead Railway. We caught the train at the Pier Head. The round trip was about thirteen miles. It was great. We went south end first to Dingle, parts of the journey being underground. We stayed on the same train to return to the north end, my father pointing out all the different ships, their probable destinations and cargoes, and those on which he had sailed. As we passed the Pier Head I saw a look of sadness and regret on his face; here we were approaching the docks where he must have joined many a ship in his seafaring days – the *Huskisson*, *Canada*, *Brocklebank*, *Alexandra* and *Gladstone*. He seemed to know every vessel and every nook and cranny. At Seaforth Sands we had to get off the train, go down a flight of stairs and wait for the train on its way back as it went to Seaforth and Litherland Station for the driver to change ends. Eventually we returned to the Pier Head. It had been one of the most interesting and memorable days of my young life.

On arriving home, we found my father's best friend sitting in the kitchen; he had just come home from sea, inquired about my father's health and had brought us kids some sweets and chocolate. He had been Dad's mate for over twenty years having served in World War I together. They went out for a pint but the next day father seemed upset and anxious, which seemed strange as such outings usually cheered him up; we at first thought he was worried about his eldest son who had just gone to train to be a chef at the Grosvenor House Hotel in London.

It proved to be more serious for this was the year that *Thetis* submarine was undergoing trials in the Mersey. Something went tragically wrong as, somehow, it

Posing with my father and brother.

got stuck and was unable to move although one end was sticking right out of water. At first people confidently thought the authorities would burn a hole in it and save all the men on board. For some reason it was not to be and the crowds kept up their vigils, knowing the crew was dying. The loss of life was absolutely appalling. It was later salvaged, renamed the *Thunderbolt* but it seemed riddled with bad luck as it never returned from active service. The debates about the whole business went on between my father and other seafarers for years, tainted with sorrow and a sneaking suspicion that not all that could have been done was.

War preparations now began in earnest for this was to be the first total war to affect civilians as well as military personnel. Some, like Mr Rooney, began to erect their Anderson shelters. Well, those lucky enough to have gardens. People earning £250 or less a year were given one free; over £250, they were charged seven pounds. People who did not have gardens had shelters built of brick put up in their back yards. If you had no room, shelters were built on the street and houses with cellars had them reinforced with steel girders.

Then the government began to issue gas masks, ration cards, stirrup pumps, steel helmets, whistles and rattles; the latter were for the Air Raid wardens who were to look after us when 'Gerry' came. Men who were on reserve from the services were called up, while others volunteered.

All this eased the unemployment situation and we teenagers felt increasingly optimistic; little did we consider the tragedies which lay ahead. My father and his mate, Jimmy Cook, went to join the Royal Navy; Jimmy was accepted but father was turned down on health grounds; he looked broken when he came home with the news. I doubt he ever got over this rejection. One of my cousins was training for the priesthood but left the seminary, again to join the Navy. By the end of the war he was a Lieutenant Commander; one of his brothers became a bomber pilot while another in the Merchant fleet was lost at sea. Aunt Julia's son, John, did his bit as a rear gunner in the RAF but was later wounded and grounded to survive the war.

Ration books then appeared on the scene, as did sand bags in the streets. ARP wardens were trained to deal with incendiary bombs and they, in turn, began to organise small groups of people to look after designated areas. School children were being prepared for evacuation to the countryside.

Then came the orders on the 'blackout'; blackout material was to be used for curtains but it was pretty difficult to get given the universal level of demand. Everyone was strictly warned that when the blackout came, any light showing would result in a heavy fine. The windows of both shops and houses were gradually covered with strips of brown, sticky paper to minimise any danger with flying glass. At nightfall, all vehicles were supposed to stop and put out their lights unless they were involved in essential work. Regulations were later issued for headlights to be covered

r which had slits to reduce the glare. It seemed a good idea but
those with poor sight; ironically, given the increase in traffic for
e number of accidents began to escalate.

like myself such changes were accepted with initial excitement but
ame the norm. It was difficult to remember life without all the para-
phernalia. I was working at Gordon's and having the time of my life. I had even
taken up dancing, despite two obstinate left feet. The local dance hall was the
'Carlton', which was, in fact little more than some rooms above a shop, King's and
Heywood's, at the corner or Bevington Hill and Scotland Road. We gave it the nick-
name of the 'Silver Slipper' as it sounded more posh and 'classy'. God, it was just
the opposite; there were always fights, superficially over the girls. It was surrounded
by pubs, the managers of which turned a blind eye to underage drinkers with coppers
in their pockets.

The favourite with teenagers was the 'Traveller's Rest' at the top of Burlington
Street and better known to us as 'Tim Foley's'. Needless to say, after a couple of
pints we were all 'on our way' and if we could not get in at the 'Slipper', we would
go to 'Peppers', a dance hall in Everton Road.

Once one acquired the necessary experience, all the good dancers or 'crack jazzers'
graduated to Blair Hall, above the Co-op in Walton Road. Then for those genuinely
interested in the foxtrot, quick step, tango and waltz, there was the 'creme de la
creme' at 'Burton's', above Burton's the Tailors, at the corner of Spellow Lane. This
indeed appeared to be the only place where people really did dance. Even Blair Hall
could erupt instantly into mayhem because of its close proximity to the 'Pacific' pub,
known as 'Arthur's', where again underage drinking was more than tolerated. Some
teenagers would pass out pints to even younger drinkers out in the street. Beer, then
as now, was the core of all the trouble.

The Liverpool stadium provided Sunday enjoyment; the boxing and wrestling
which had previously been scheduled for the evening was moved to an afternoon
slot. It put on some excellent shows, with many local lads making their names. Two
I will always remember were Joe Curran, who later fought Jackie Patterson for a
title, and Billy Hardacre. The latter's dad had a little gym in the back yard of their
house in Penrhyn Street where he taught all his sons the true art of boxing. I still
feel, if the war had not come, Billy could have been a great professional and possibly
had reached the top. He still lives in his father's house and is probably the man
whom politicians should consult about the problems of the inner cities; he has been
all his life a shining example of a good citizen.

Sundays were also days for the cinemas in town; our favourites were the
'Majestic', the 'Paramount' (now the 'Odeon'), the 'Forum', 'Scala' and the
'Futurist'. As often as not, there were queues to get in for the 'big picture'; the times

for the latter were prominently displayed but, as they had continuous performances, you could go in at any time you liked, seats permitting. Indeed, some elderly folk often slept through at least two performances, either for the warmth or simply because they had nowhere else to go.

There was a whole host of dirty tricks in which one could indulge to get seats; if, for example, the commissioner shouted, 'One seat only!' a mate might rush in, get installed and then drop a bad egg (acquired usually from Melias food stores in Virgil Street). This was worse than any manufactured stink bomb; seats would quickly be vacated and in would come the rest of the gang, now all sitting together. The smell would be endured for a while. The same trick was often pulled at crowded football grounds where it often resulted in some terrible abuse and the occasional witty remark but still produced the desired effect.

By 1939, a fourth and final brother was born but things seemed much more prosperous with father and three of us in work, one still being in London. As people's spending power increased, there seemed to be more parties or 'dos' on Saturday nights; perhaps it was just our age and the worry of war. I well remember one; having been to Tim Foley's and, of course, the 'Silver Slipper', two girls asked us back to their house in Hopwood Street where the family were having a farewell 'do' for a son about to join the army. The house turned out to be one of the nice council houses at the top of the street on the left looking towards the docks. By the time we got there, the place was swinging, front door wide open, piano music and singing thumping down the lobby. The place was packed but the girls got us a bottle of 'Walker's S/B' beer as we remarked on the heavenly smell of food coming from the kitchen. The girls took us through and we passed an 'ole gerl' sitting regally in a rocking chair in a black furrier shawl and eating something from a plate.

'She's gorra beard, look, look!' the pal exclaimed in horror.

'Oh, get lost – you've had too much ale.'

'No, honest, look. She's got a bloody beard!'

Sure enough, the old one looked like a circus exhibit. On entering the kitchen, we found out why. In addition to plenty of fresh bread, there in a galvanised bath bubbling away on the top of a very posh gas stove was mountains of sticky, delicious pigs' feet. Thus as the poor old dear turned her head, the juice was dribbling down her chin and catching the hair from her shawl. Not that we managed to consume them with any greater aplomb.

More and more 'dos' began spontaneously; if people were in 'good company' in a pub on a Saturday, near closing time a house would be volunteered and a kitty organised. A few crates of beer would be duly purchased, along with usually a few quart bottles of mild and bitter, so liquid refreshment was generally inexpensive.

People were extraordinarily good at providing their own entertainment in a pre-technological age. Many could play the piano, mouth organ, accordion, banjo or spoons and everyone, regardless of voice, had 'their' song. Some were extremely talented and far more professional than the full timers at the music halls. Eventually, the gramophone began to make its appearance, for good or ill. Now we even have the music videos *et al* and I do think it is sad that a decreasing number of people can entertain themselves and others but, as with food, have to rely on the processed variety.

Thus Saturdays, after a week in Gordon's provided the best enjoyment of the week with the added bonus of a 'lie in' on Sundays.

Yet one fateful Sunday, father woke me for Mass and smelt beer on my breath. There was hell to pay. He went berserk and told me while I lived in his house he was the boss and I had to make sure I kept my nose clean. An uneasy atmosphere lingered for days and I made sure he never caught me out again. Sometimes rows would break out over Mass itself, as by this point I and the brothers had become hardened cynics about organised religion.

Father himself rarely went, but insisted we did. When we pointed this out we received a similar retort, i.e. that while we were under his roof we obeyed his rules. I must admit we quite admired him for it, albeit tinged with some sullen resentment. If father was not shouting you out of bed for church, the Salvation Army would drive you slowly mad, marching round the streets and forcing hymns down reluctant ears. I regarded them as my first encounter with noise pollution but eventually they suffered so much abuse, that they confined themselves to certain street corners and left the rest of us in grateful peace.

Nevertheless, Sunday boredom did have its dark side; with church attendance falling and with more cash for Sunday lunchtime sessions, there seemed to be more potential for fights and brawls. From such fights, men earned reputations as 'hard knocks', although not all were louts; some were real gentlemen who were ready to restore order and put the rougher element in its place. Such were 'Hoot' and Sam Gibson, two brothers who never looked for trouble but heaven help any yob who crossed them. 'Hoot' went into the army and became the heavyweight champion; after the war he would later display his gold medal with pride on his waistcoat. The last time I saw him he was in the Corp of Commissioners, doing duty at Everton football ground. Sam went into the Merchant Navy and the last time we met he was collecting for the Sisters of Charity; by then, his sight was failing but both retained their fearless yet gentle characters.

Conversations were increasingly dominated by the prospect of war, although all welcomed the improvements in jobs. I only knew one guy who was made temporarily redundant by Hitler; he was the local gas lamp lighter, but he seemed quite pleased by the whole thing as he said he was 'fed up carrying the bloody ladder

Central Station.

round for years in all weathers'. The council found him another job and, so, the lamps went out in Scottie in 1939, to return in June 1944. Gas light stayed till the 1950s, when it was gradually replaced by electricity.

September 1939 brought the forlorn sight of evacuees leaving Liverpool, crying their eyes out at railway stations with their little cardboard boxes for their gas masks; some had small cases for belongings, most carried paper bundles. Thus, nationally, about three and a half million kids were moved mainly from industrial areas into the country, all with the best possible intentions, if not results.

As far as Scottie was concerned, it seemed like ninety-five per cent of them were back within three months, although some did move out again in 1941 and 1942. In normal circumstances I doubt if anyone ever considered leaving the area.

The kick-off for World War Two was officially 3 September 1939 but civilians lived through a strange period of phoney war before their collective struggle began. Nevertheless, it was not long before the Germans got their first victims at sea which sparked off emotions in Scottie best kept suppressed. Within hours of Chamberlain's declaration, the *Athenia*, a ship bound for Canada with women and children, was sunk by a German U-boat. It appeared the U-boat gave no warning as had been customary during World War One.

When the news reached Scotland Road, hatred and prejudice, fed by months of waiting, erupted. It was fuelled by the fact that a good many families had seafaring

Netherfield Road, with steps leading up to Sampson Street. (LIV.R.O.)

interests or sons and brothers in the services. I remember standing with some mates at the top of 'Bosi' when we saw a huge crowd coming up Scottie from Byrom Street; there were hundreds of them. Their main purpose was to wreck any shop bearing an Italian or German name. It was frightening to behold the mob. Falavio's, between Doncaster and Athol Streets, was the first I saw attacked; I had bought many an ice cream there. Shops were torn apart. The crowd then headed down Taylor Street and along Great Homer towards the market. We dashed down 'Bosi' and through the entries to warn our old pal, the German butcher at the bottom of Newsham Street. We banged almost hysterically at his door but could get no answer. Within minutes the mob arrived; the shop was empty but they wrecked it all the same.

The odd thing was that people did not seem interested in pinching the food or any actions that might be seen as looting; they just seemed bent on destruction. Next came Falavio's second shop, between Chapel Gardens and Penryhn Street. Outside the shop, hanging between the bedroom windows, was one of the saddest sights I have seen in my life – a Union Jack about six foot by four, with the words, 'I have a son serving in the RAF', written on it. It was no good; there was no controlling them now. The flag was torn to shreds, as was everything else. The same fate awaited another German pork butcher at the corner of Wilbraham Street. Throughout this riot I never saw one policeman, which was perhaps just as well, as anyone trying to talk sense might have been lynched.

The next day was, however, a different story; the crowd had missed one shop in its carnage, Rossetta's, an Italian chippie between Howe and Buckingham Streets. The Black Maria was there, as Rossetta herself plus several large cases and heavily protected by the police was escorted into the van. She was, by God, defiant as before finally getting into the 'Maria', she put down her cases and gave the Hitler salute. The crowd went berserk but the police quite literally threw her into the vehicle accompanied by a cheer from the mob. The next day we went to Athol Street police station to enquire about our dear old friend, the pork butcher; all we wanted to know was if he was safe but the Sergeant informed us haughtily that 'he's gone on holiday and what's it to you?' We asked where he had gone and then the officer got very touchy and informed us, 'If you persist in your enquiries, I will have to report you and this may result in imprisonment for aiding the enemy!'

What a load of tripe! Needless to say we took his 'advice' and left pretty sharpish. We never saw the old German again, though later we heard that 'aliens' had been interned on the Isle of Man. I still hope he had a reasonable 'holiday' because I doubt very much if he would have been any good to Hitler.

The war, such as it was at that point, seemed to be confined to sea. It was all bad news as far as we were concerned. Both the aircraft carrier, *Courageous*, and the battleship, *The Royal Oak*, were sunk at sea with dreadful loss of life. The only good news we had was that the German battleship, the *Graf Spee*, had been trapped by the Royal Navy but it had turned and fled to Montevideo in December 1939. Scotland Road was full of it waiting for the news that it had left port and had been captured by the Royal Navy but it was not to be. The German captain, Langdorf was ordered by Hitler to scuttle his ship to prevent it falling into enemy hands. The captain duly obliged, released his crew and the prisoners he held and then took his own life. All this deeply affected many in Scottie, as the captain soared in their respect and admiration, not least when the prisoners confirmed they had been very well treated.

Although we heard more and more tragic stories, life still went on as normal. Many people seemed to be disappearing into the services; barrage balloons appeared in the sky attached to heavy steel cables which in turn were clamped to military vehicles. The Air Force chaps would winch them up and down for regular testing. The air raid sirens were subjected to similar practice runs, all waiting for something to happen.

Gordon's warehouse, where I worked, was by this point crammed to capacity with food, as were all the shops owned by the firm. New deliveries came daily, but

A land mine in 1941 demolished most of the area around this area of Anthony Street and Netherfield Road. This photograph dates from 1948. (LIV.R.O.)

Scotland Road in 1908. When the building in the centre of this view was demolished, the local 'Ollie' championships were held on the open ground for many years. Streets used to compete and bets were always placed on the outcome. A petrol station now fills the site. (LIV.R.O.)

there were even structural problems with the warehouse floors given the sheer weight of it all. The whole place began to creak ominously. The stocks, however, never lasted that long, as hysterical rumours abounded about the imminence of rationing. These obviously had the desired effect and some suppliers and grocers must have made a packet in the process.

Rationing was eventually introduced on 8 January 1940 on butter, bacon, ham and sugar. Other sorts of meat had to wait till March. In some ways it was a damned good job it came in the January as, by then, unofficial rationing was already hitting those without the money or contacts. Apart from meat, most commodities were rationed by weight, the biggest blow being two ounces of tea per person. Nevertheless rationing at least had the advantage of being just and fair.

By June 1941 clothes were rationed according to a points system. Obviously some items did not come on ration but still became rare and difficult to acquire. This led to such goods going 'under the counter' or on the black market. Quite a few shopkeepers encouraged this, some to give preferential treatment to their regulars, others, as usual, out of sheer greed.

Newspaper circulation must have increased one hundred per cent for, as regular customers asked for a paper, the shopkeeper would quickly wrap some precious cigarettes *et al* in it. Sometimes this backfired when a buyer genuinely only wanted a paper but no one seemed to notice the server's embarrassment. All this lasted until well after the war and applied to items such as combs, razor blades, pens and pencils. Some wise characters deliberately began to call at various shops and pubs to become 'regulars'.

The real fun started when clothes and then sweets were rationed by a coupon system in which only the shopkeeper was supposed to remove the coupons from the book. It was illegal to accept loose coupons and government inspectors were quite vigilant in prosecuting local traders during the early part of the war. Some occupational groups were allowed extra clothing rations such as seafarers and those employed in heavy manual work. Yet despite the efforts of the inspectorate, clothes coupons were easily sold for one and sixpence to two shillings and sixpence each. There were plenty of buyers.

Some shops began to adopt the so-called 'quota system' and thus sell their scarce commodities in a matter of hours if not minutes. Huge queues would assemble only to hear the owner announce that he was sold out. No one ever seemed to mind but put it down to bad luck. Queues could form instantly, people not even knowing or caring as to what was on sale. Some kids had a good time by pretending to form a queue outside a shop and watch unsuspecting adults follow suit. Many shopkeepers were fined for all this, as were street traders who were known to the police and arrested with tiresome regularity. Black marketeering seemed to reach its peak in 1943, with some relaxation in prosecutions. Perhaps the authorities decided to turn a blind eye. The obvious image of the war was the disappearance of park railings but one thing always struck me as comical and really typical of the time; although the parks, naked of rails, were left surrounded by small brick walls, the huge gates remained and they were still opened and locked at set times, no doubt the result of some meaningless, bureaucratic brainwave.

Thus by spring 1940, many people found themselves quite enjoying the war; nothing had happened to most families except a boost in paid employment and an apparently fairer distribution of essential goods. The black market in scarcities and the prosecutions merely added a touch of zest to the whole proceedings. Little did we realise how things would have changed by Christmas!

Chapter Eight

A Liverpool war

It was not until 25 June 1940 that the first real air raid siren was sounded over Liverpool; momentarily, everyone stood still in amazement. Then some dashed to their shelters while we, full of youthful bravado and curiosity, waited at the top of 'Bosi' to see if we could spot any Gerry planes and to be ready to offer assistance. We were pleasantly surprised by the 'all clear'; nothing bad happened. Indeed it would be a further two months, 17 August to be precise, before the first bomb dropped on the city. Life even then went on, reflecting the typical catchphrase, 'business as usual'.

I found, given my position at Gordon's, that I was acquiring a lot of 'friends'; some of whom definitely hoped for 'goodies' in the form of blown and damaged tins of fruit which in peace time were thrown away. (I wished I could have known this as a kid!) I also noticed the increasing number of well-dressed visitors who began to frequent the warehouse; this would have been unknown before rationing. Most would leave with parcels in their chauffeur-driven cars; they even used to acknowledge my presence, which again would have been abnormal in 1939. The whole set-up seemed to stink but I was happy in the job I had and had the good sense not to question the behaviour of these local dignitaries, all of whom had respected positions in so-called 'society' and most of whom had the hypocrisy to lecture others on the need to tighten belts whenever they were given the chance. As far as I was concerned, I did my best to do the same for my real friends who had suffered enough in the 'thirties.

Daft as it sounds, we were all looking forward to Christmas 1940; so far it had been one of the best years of my life; I felt really good and seemed to have no worries, but it was not to last. I think I was one of the few people to pay any attention to the announcement of Neville Chamberlain's death on 9 November. Most had no good to say of the man save that he had been kidded by the greatest con-man in history. I never really believed this although 'peace in our time' was, with hindsight, an unfortunate phrase. As far as I was concerned, Chamberlain's 'appeasement' provided Britain with a few valuable months to prepare for the inevitable.

On 20 November the sirens sounded again, this time for real. The bombing lasted for three nights; the devastation was more than we were prepared for, although, to be fair, everyone kept their cool. The real blow came with the news that about three hundred and fifty people had lost their lives. The frustrating thing seemed to be that

Bomb damage photographed from Derby Square. (LIV.R.O.)

there was nothing we could do about it, nor it appeared, could the service people. We felt victimised and unprotected, like defenceless animals.

They did have these 'smoke screen' machines, belching out black smoke all over the place; these ingenious monstrosities were supposed to hinder Gerry pilots and stop them hitting their set targets. God only knows if they worked; we just seemed to get bombed instead! They added insult to injury if the wind blew the accursed smoke in your face; you would be temporarily blinded and would probably cough for hours.

After that, we had a temporary reprieve to internalise our baptism of bombing before it all started again, on 28 November. This time the bombers dropped flares which lit up the sky. It really was more eerie than the bombing itself. Little did we realise that we were about to be introduced to the landmine. These floated down on us by parachute, usually made of a green material; they were essentially sea mines and when they exploded they blasted outwards destroying everything within a set distance. The old houses literally just vanished leaving in their wake a heap of rubble. In my opinion, they were the worst devices used to bomb Liverpool.

Still, Christmas was coming and most people tried to put this horror behind them;

our spirits never failed and I think for many it was a true learning experience, witnessing their own stamina and that of their neighbours. Indeed, human beings are so adaptable in that most just got on with it, accepting changing conditions as a variety of norms.

Then came 21 December. God, what a night! The community was in uproar as the 'bloody Gerries' hit St Anthony's Church and School. The priest naturally got an immediate gang of volunteers to help to put out the flames on the church roof. By now we were all learning how to get organised instantly there was a hit. We began to make sure there were plenty of sandbags available, as these were the most effective in dealing with incendiary bombs as the latter, though destructive, were only small, about fifteen inches long and two inches in diameter.

During this particular raid, I did a really stupid trick; in my keenness I noticed one of these 'fire bombs' spurting away; I picked up a sand bag and dashed towards it. I ran, smack, bang, right into the back of a parked lorry, a Walker's milk lorry naturally without lights. When I regained consciousness, I had a very badly bruised face and swore there and then that some Gerry would pay for this! I never carried a sandbag again. The next morning at work the jokes went thick and fast at my expense. I never knew if I'd even put the bloody bomb out.

Those who were bombed soon found accommodation with family or friends or by the council which had lists of properties vacated by families who had left the city, some returning to their native Wales. Private landlords were delighted to re-let such property, not only for the rent but for the protection it afforded. The people worst placed were those who had to leave their homes because of unexploded bombs. They could not be rehoused even temporarily, as they were not strictly speaking homeless, yet they could be kept waiting for disposal.

Some bombs contained delay mechanisms while others were flawed. Whatever the case, the whole area would be evacuated. (The most 'high explosive' bombs dropped, apart from landmines, weighed about 500lbs.) After the war, I watched the demolition of some great buildings and warehouses as the city suffered industrial decline; some took a hammering before they eventually fell and, with hindsight, it struck me that these would have afforded much better protection than the hastily erected street shelters the local populace was given. Most would never use them, except as urinals; consequently, they stank; in contrast the great warehouses had anything from ten to sixteen floors with a foot of concrete or brick between each floor. A 500lb bomb could not have got through more than three floors; indeed, some office staff began to realise this and eventually made their homes in the ground and basement floors. The Americans, too, were very clever when they arrived, for they picked the Stanley warehouse as one of their main store depots. It still stands, maybe for historical reasons or maybe the Yanks still own it. The government was

A postcard of Church Street in the city centre. (LIV.R.O.)

certainly aware of the potential of these structures as, throughout the war, the Admiralty used one of the basements for the HQ responsible for controlling all the shipping in the Atlantic, in the 'Western Approaches'.

Despite the bombing of St Anthony's, or perhaps because of it, everyone was determined to enjoy Christmas, come what may. The church was packed as usual for Midnight Mass on Christmas Eve; the congregation was not exclusively Catholic and there was a genuine sense of true Christmas spirit in the soaring voices of 'Peace on earth, good will to all men.' After Mass most families had a table of food ready for a midnight feast, accompanied by plenty of drink. It proved to be the best Christmas I have ever had; I had been able to buy all the family presents and my father even let us have an alcoholic drink in the house. Like a lot of other parents, he seemed to realise that the war was making us grow up abnormally quickly and there was this general feeling of 'here today, gone tomorrow'. Two of the first lads from 'Bosi' had been killed on active service, John Flaherty, a local carter and John Loftus, our local 'bookie'. Both had everything to live for, rest in peace.

By the New Year of 1941, things were becoming scarce. Shops began to close with all the restrictions. Gordon's, however, seemed to be going from strength to strength. I was still doing the Saturday morning collections with my employers; my wages doubled and I was asked to fire watch the warehouse every other Sunday from 8 a.m. till 6 p.m. Never once while I did this did the sirens wail. My birthday was approaching and I could feel that both at home and at work surprises were being planned for me. Sure enough, the office girls and the warehouse staff bought me two ties and two shirts while I got a watch and a pair of shoes from my parents.

I was having an excellent time until the news came over the radio that the battleship HMS *Hood* (42,000 tons) had been sunk with only three survivors from a crew of fourteen hundred men. The date was 23 March 1941. Father's mate, Jimmy Cook, was on board. Father went out and got plastered; he returned disturbed and violently angry. He was convinced Jimmy was dead and the news was confirmed by a visit from Jim's brother. Although I never saw my father drunk again, it took him months to get over his loss, if indeed, he ever did.

In view of the growing scarcities, the Government then opened the 'British Restaurant' in Byrom Street, a few doors from one of our firm's shops. Much to the annoyance of local cafés, the food was marvellous in this non-profit-making cafeteria; meat and fish with two veg for six old pence, puddings or sweets at three-pence, soup for five pence and tea, coffee or cocoa for a penny. Thus you could have a three-course meal for one shilling and tuppence. People took advantage of the place, eating there regularly and saving up their rations for the weeks.

The Government tried to entice us with all kinds of novel foodstuffs to alleviate shortages, though whalemeat and tuna never captured imaginations in 'Scottie'. White bread was replaced by wholemeal, while potatoes, thankfully, were never rationed. When the Americans arrived, so too did dried egg, dried veg and the ubiquitous Spam.

Tuesday, 1 May 1941, despite the events of the previous Christmas, still came as a traumatic shock. When the sirens sounded, at first no one took much notice for there had been so many false alarms. Even when we heard the planes there were innumerable smart alecs who claimed they were ours, 'I can tell by the engines' became an instant catchphrase. Then we saw them and soon after the first massive explosions.

The docks appeared alit with fires. Timber yards went up immediately and the screeching of the bombs reduced humans and animals to temporary terror. Some were even saying daft things like if you heard the screeching, you were safe. Scottie Road was full of dust, broken glass, peculiar nauseous smells and, much to the kids' delight after the raid, glistening, jagged, highly-coloured shrapnel. It all lasted for well over five bewildering hours.

When we heard the 'all clear' the general consensus was that it could never be as bad again, but we were wrong, oh so wrong. The next night Gerry was back again and it was far worse. People rapidly began to move out of the city centre and dock areas, mainly to get some sleep, for most would be back at work soon after the 'all clear.'

The third night was the high point; Gerry sent all available planes. The figures vary but it seems certain that the city was hit by between 500 and 750 planes carrying absolutely everything, bombs, mines, incendiaries. I honestly thought Liverpool would burn down, lock, stock and barrel, that night. Everywhere there was flying glass and debris. The noise and the smells were indescribable; the SS *Malakind*, an ammunition ship in Huskisson Dock, caught fire and had to be abandoned because of the intense heat. When it blew, its contents scattered for miles. The market and Cazeneau Street took several hits. The loss of life affected many; a friend went searching for another pal only to be found several hours later on top of a crater cradling what was left of his mate's head.

The next day Hitler's voice of propaganda, dear old Lord Haw Haw, alias William Joyce, had the nerve to announce over the wireless that there were riots in Scotland Road. What a load of rubbish. Even those who had hitched rides on lorries at the Rotunda to country areas were back by the morning, as often as not to see rubble where their homes had stood. Fires lingered everywhere, gas mains exploded and worst of all was the shortage of water. The Government sent 2,600 troops to the city to help out and to stop any outbreaks of looting.

The fourth and fifth nights were re-runs of the previous three but on the Saturday I found out why my employers had trained me to come on the collections. The drive

Johnnie Woods in uniform.

was not surprisingly difficult given all the debris and detours. The car driven by the boss's son proceeded slowly down Bevington Hill, Gardner's Row and then into Fontenoy Street. Here we were turned back by a policeman and we went down Marybone. The car then stopped and I was handed the keys to the shop in Byrom Street and told to use the back entrance. I got out and ducked under a rope across Henry Edward Street and ran across Fontenoy Street into Fontenoy Gardens. I opened the rear door and it was then it struck me how silent everywhere was. While searching for the cash box, I glanced across to the 'Morning Star' pub opposite. In between was a gent's toilet with railings and there, blowing on the railings, was an ominous green parachute, a landmine! I made a speedy exit going back on my tracks when I noticed a cracked pavement in Henry Edward Street; there sticking up at an acute angle were the 'fins' of an unexploded bomb.

At this point I was ordered to stop by a bobby, accompanied by an air raid warden and two well-dressed members of the local CID. Back at the rope I hurriedly explained my business and the CID insisted on speaking to the boss's son. He got the telling-off of his life!

None of my employers ever apologised for the danger in which they had know-ingly placed me but I never went on the Saturday run again and Rooney, when he heard, came close to drawing blood and losing his job. Indeed I had to restrain him. I went home to grab a few hours' kip before fire watching on the Sunday but Saturday night brought what seemed by now its routine visit by the Luftwaffe. After fire watching on the Sunday, I had my tea and went down to Tim Foley's for a couple of pints and then back to the top of 'Bosi' to await our unwelcome visitors. This time an old lady, Mrs Bradley, who lived on her own next door to Joe Allen's, received a calling card in the shape of an incendiary. She had refused to go into the shelters throughout the bombing but the bomb was stuck in the rafters and within seconds someone broke down her front door and ran up to the attic. With her home on the verge of destruction, she stayed in her rocking chair commenting: 'They should have burned these bloody houses down years ago, they're so bleedin' cold.' In the background, Liverpool was ablaze.

The Gerries had a field day, with little or no opposition. With all the flares they had dropped, the pilots probably knew the city better than the average Scouser. On Monday 7 May the bastards dropped incendiaries on the Rotunda. There was little water and, as it stood at the junction of Stanley and Kirkdale Roads, the wind fanned the flames. It went down like a glorious Spanish galleon in the greatest grand finale of all time, never to be seen again. The 'all-clear' finally sounded at 4.30 a.m. on the morning of 8 May, the end of the May blitz. The destruction had been beyond imagination, the statistics coldly portraying human misery, 1,453 recorded dead, 1,056 injured.

After the mayhem, the tales of the blitz abounded, some witty, some not. O'Hare's pawnshop had been hit by an incendiary bomb, people rushed in to salvage pledged possessions before the fire took hold; everything from suits to musical instruments were showered into the street; it took a few weeks for some fellows to find their suits.

Some streets had fire alarms at the corner, one being at Newsham Street; when Mrs Bradley's was hit, some idiotic drunk kept insisting on using this alarm to summon the fire engines; it had completely escaped his consciousness that the whole city was on fire.

One place which did good trade throughout the mayhem was the 'Champion Weights' lodging house at the top of Taylor Street; here you could get a bed for sixpence a night; down in the cellar the beds lined the walls but in the middle of the room was a rope surrounded by benches; again here men would sit and rest head and arms on the rope in search of sleep.

The night Great Mersey Street was hit by a landmine, the dairy at the corner of Lambeth and Stanley Roads had its gates blasted open; the cows sedately walked along Stanley Road, some wags commenting they must have come from the 'Grosvenor' which was showing a cowboy film.

In the same way Harper's stables had been hit, resulting in the huge carthorses running wild around the streets. The thing that really still upsets me is when people say Liverpool wanted to surrender; absolute tosh! Perhaps the troops sent in to assist might have added to the confusion here by seeing slogans such as 'No surrender' belonging to older battles, as the populace of Belfast still testify. Again slogan painters added to the general confusion; I remember seeing a guy paint on a wall in a pub in Netherfield Road 'Down with the Pope'. By the next day 'the' had been erased and some comic had added 'ye' to 'Pope'. Outsiders like the troops must have thought we were real queer heels to have something in for Popeye!

Both during and after the blitz, the beer shortage became severe. Men relentlessly tried to get information as to which pub had stocks and when they would be sold. A stampede up and down Scottie would ensue when such information became general knowledge. 'Guinness' was scarce right into the 'fifties and whisky and other spirits tended to disappear 'under the counter.' The latter was very expensive and when the Americans developed a taste for such stuff, they were mercilessly exploited by some pub managers. One guy in particular made a fortune from our Allies by filling clear bottles with two inches of 'overproof' rum topped up with water. The Yanks lapped it up at five pounds a bottle. He did have problems getting clear bottles, though, for which he would pay a shilling each.

Nowadays Liverpool, perhaps for political reasons, seems to attract more than its share of bad media publicity. They all choose to forget the city's positive contributions throughout this century. During the war, for instance, towns competed to raise cash for the war effort, Liverpool coming top with eleven and a half million pounds. We supplied more than enough servicemen and women, many of whom never returned. Maybe our quick wits and sharp articulation frighten outsiders, although most comment on the hospitality and humour they encounter on their visits. I think what puts a lot of politicians off us is that we don't suffer fools gladly and tell them so!

After the May blitz, life thankfully quietened down and some resumed their usual pastimes such as fighting and brawling. To be fair, a special policeman nicknamed 'Blackie' did his best to keep order, always being prepared to have a go, despite his small stature. We left 'Bosi' in November 1941 and moved to a better house in Olivia Street; I never, though, got to know anyone here; my old habits and haunts were too well ingrained. Christmas 1942 came and went and my birthday promised to be good, with the staff at Gordon's as generous as ever. Yet when I came home, my mother said father was in bed; although not drunk, he had been drinking heavily on the anniversary of Jimmy Cook's death. I went out for a pint and, on my return, found him sitting at the table; I asked him how he was and he just blew a fuse, ranting and raving about Jimmy; I tried to talk some sense but made matters worse and as I retreated to bed I was stung by his parting blow:

'If yer don't like it here, you can always leave!'

I brooded on this all the next day at work, two brothers were now away from home and perhaps, given my father's mood, it was time I went. The idea caught hold and soon after I packed my bag, explained to my upset mother and set off for work down south. I must have been mad.

Eventually I ended up on a building site in Felixstowe but could not settle. I missed Scottie but felt it was too soon to go home, tail between my legs. I caught a train to Ipswich, had a couple of pints and walked into a recruiting office. In a desire to prove myself to my father, I joined the army. I then felt I could go home to await my call-up; everyone, especially at Gordon's, was really friendly. Even Dad never mentioned the row again. I then had my last night out in Scottie, little realising how long it would be before I returned. The next day I caught the train to Euston, changing for Waterloo and then into Norwich. I asked a military policeman the way to Brittania Barracks and he nodded me towards an army lorry.

'Are yer going to Brittania Barracks?' I asked.

'Yes, worse bloody luck!' came the reply.

What a reception ... but that's another story.

Notes to the text

Chapter One – The street

1. 'Joe Allen's' later became known as 'Fitzies' and 'Duffy's' and 'Ma Russell's' or the 'Europa'.
2. Jack Perry who had a couple of ponies and carts owned one, the other belonging to the Booths.
3. Later known as Rankin's.
4. The people I remember most were Mrs Bradley, the Owens, Woodfalls, Wilsons, Doyles, Duffys, Collins, Ainsworths, Boardmans, Welshs, Loftus, Allens, Crumbies, Wignalls, Duckworths, Fishers, Polands, Delahuntys, Potts, Devereux, Carrolls, Fynns, Flahertys, Cresswells, Horans, Rooneys, Mullens, Dixons, Rankins, Parrys, Booths, Rileys, McGivens, Kinsellas, Keatings, Nicholsons and Rimmers.
5. The 'entries' were the alleys between houses and streets, allowing access to the back yards.
6. By 1939 there were five of us, Georgie, Martin, Frank, Chris and myself, Joseph dying in infancy thanks largely to the greed of our local medical practitioner in the days before NHS provision.
7. He had been a 'navvie', digging roads and laying drains and took ill after years of working without proper clothing in all weathers; breaks were unheard of even in the worst weather, the very suggestion could result in the 'sack' and the 'dole' queues were teeming with potential replacements.

Chapter Two – Early days at school

1. My elementary school was divided into infants, juniors and seniors but, for status, we preferred the term 'big boys' for the latter.
2. The 'A' stream was taught by Miss Atkinson.
3. The shop stood between Hopwood and Doncaster Streets.
4. Needless to say, I never took it up but still have an urge to draw.
5. This outfit was to last for years, being worn only on Sundays for Mass.
6. A stirring cart was just a piece of wood about five feet long and nine inches wide, with a wooden box nailed on top, all being placed on four old pram wheels on axles. The back axle with two wheels was nailed rigid, the front one was attached to a four-inch by twelve-inch piece of wood which had a hole burned in the centre, as did the main plank of the stirrie proper with a nut and bolt joining the two together; this was allowed to swivel, a rope being placed around the wood on the front wheels and inside each wheel the rope was tied to make a kind of rein. These carts were our main form of transporting stuff.

7. The 'Tunnel of Love' was a popular courting spot for office workers who had a cuddle with their partners before catching trains after work.

8. One of the gang lived with his grandmother in 'Bosi', and she let us use her cellar as our club for years.

Chapter Three – Pawnshops and poverty

1. He represented Scotland Road for as long as anyone could remember. He must have been the only MP who had to go through his back yard to get to his front door.

2. A local cinema.

3. Known to us as 'Lee Jones'.

Chapter Four – 'You've got to earn a penny or two!'

1. The new St Anne's police headquarters now stands in roughly the same spot today.

2. It is now in Great Homer Street.

3. I later found out that the giblets were also in great demand by local hotels for soups and pates.

4. I always knew Mr Ginsberg as 'I'. Presumably his first name was Isaac.

5. This was still in the days when Roman Catholics fasted from midnight on Saturday if they were going to Communion.

6. My father had retired from the sea by this point.

7. £1 15s. 0d. per week.

8. On my way to work that day I always remember finding a purse by the tram lines at the junction of Scottie and Cazeneau Street. I was going to hand it to the policeman there on duty but he shouted at me to clear the lines. When I got to work Rooney and I searched it for an address but all there was were pawn tickets (19) Dalish's 218 Great Homer Street, three halfpennies, one penny and two holy medals. I returned it to the pawn shop but never heard any more.

9. These were made of corrugated steel, six foot high, four and a half feet wide and six and a half feet long; when assembled, they looked like tunnels with one end blocked, the other having a door and they would be sunk three or four feet into the garden and then covered with soil or sandbags for further protection.

Chapter Five – 'Boys will be boys'

1. This stood behind the Burlington cinema which was later to become the Tate and Lyle social club.

2. Despite its chamber of horrors reputation, the clinic was often used as a dodge to miss lessons, as one produced a yellow appointment card to skip school. Then the usual ploy was to miss your appointment by going to the toilet and so you were 'forced' to wait until the end.

3. The Rotunda.

4. Formerly a cinema.

5. Most claimed to have at least one.

6. He later moved to the other side of St Anthony's Church.

7. Much later in life when I was courting my wife, her mother eventually allowed me in for tea. I stood in horror in the kitchen as my future father-in-law, Michael Daly himself, laughed heartily and shook my hand.

8. The so-called 'penny return'.

9. The 'cast-iron shore', now Otterspool Prom.

10. Obviously there were no washing machines; everything was boiled either on coal fires in the kitchen or, in some homes, cast iron boilers. Again, some had mangles.

11. Now Gladstone Dock and Freeport.

12. Travelling by tram was not the most glamorous form of transport. The noise was quite incredible as the steel wheels rolled along the steel tracks, while the vehicle stopped and started and rattled on its way. Most in the 1930s had only wooden seats but later, the luxurious 'Green Goddesses' were introduced that had leatherette seating.

13. Lorry tyres were not easy to acquire as people with children used their rubber to sole and heel their families' boots and shoes.

14. Later in life, whenever I did not have a job that required work on Saturday afternoons, I regularly followed the team. My wife and daughter found purchasing my season ticket an instant solution to the headache of getting me a birthday present.

15. A friend has recently provided me with information about his time at St Edward's Orphanage from 1923 until 1934:

    Thingwall Hall was left as a legacy to the Liverpool Catholic Diocese by a spinster on the understanding that it be used as a retreat and home for orphans. The Christian Brothers of St Edward were given the task of turning the hall into an orphanage, hence its later name. A big extension was added, comprising of living quarters, dormitories and a dining room for sixty children. The demand for places was so great that four further buildings were eventually added, each with room for sixty children.

    Two Christian Brothers were attached to each 'cottage' and they taught the children during the day. There were also Christian Brothers in charge of the farm, the kitchen, the bakery, the laundry, the cobbler's shop, the tailor's shop, the band and, last but not least, was the Supervisor plus a resident chaplain. The band even had its own professor of music who was very religious and devoted his life to the orphanage; his name was Mr J. McKenna, known to all boys as 'Old Jack'. The brother who taught the top class was again an ex-professor, known at the home as Brother Arden, although his 'civvy' name was Professor McFall. The band consisted of thirty musicians but there was always a back-up team if required. The same was true of the football team. Every three years, boys were sent out to Canada, to the wheat belt of Manitoba to learn farming skills on government farms; after they passed their agricultural apprenticeships' they could go anywhere they wished to seek work. Such departures were always sad times for us all; before the boys went, we all got an hour off school to say our goodbyes. As the coach approached, the head brother would give a farewell speech and the band would play some of their favourite marches. The last tune before departure was 'St Edward Forever'. Then, as the coach moved off, instead of three cheers, we would shout three times, as loud as we could, 'St Edward's Forever! St Edward's Forever! St Edward's Forever!'

    When I first went to the home, it was out in the country, standing in forty-six acres of picturesque farm and grazing land. Marked out were two small, schoolboy football pitches plus a full-sized professional pitch, where the first team trained with an old leather case ball with eighteen panels. This was the secret of our success as, when the boys played at Everton's or Liverpool's grounds, they were used to their size and knew just how hard to hit the ball.

Alas, things have changed and most of the land has been sold. Part of it is now a home and school for epileptics and handicapped boys. The Christian Brothers, like my fond memories, remain.

16. Some say the 'Electra' could be classed as a 'picture house' because in its last days it showed pictures on magic lanterns, the 'thirties version of projector and slides.

17. To those unfamiliar with the war, Lord Haw-Haw was William Joyce, Hitler's propagandist 'disc jockey'!

Chapter Six – Life for the grown-ups

1. The mission hall was later refurbished and taken over by Mitchell's, a bakery firm that sold the most delicious cakes.

2. Half a pint or 23 centilitres.

3. By the glass.

4. One of these was the 'Westmorland', nicknamed the 'Honky Tonk'. Here Billy Morley was always available to 'tickle the ivories', much to everyone's enjoyment.

5. Street bookmakers were against the law. The Jacks (CID) were always trying to catch and fine them. I had saved my guardian on several occasions by spotting 'Jacks' and taking from him any betting slips – no slips, no evidence. The 'Jacks' eventually tumbled to this and would arrive in fours, fives, even sixes, to catch anyone else involved. We kids were also lectured by our local bobbies. The bookies themselves realised the predicament they had created and dispensed with our services and began to employ adult 'dowzees'.

6. I am told that Jean Alexander, better known as *Coronation Street*'s Hilda Ogden once worked there.